THE VIENNA CONVENTION ON THE LAW OF TREATIES

THE MELLAND SCHILL LECTURES
delivered at the University of Manchester
and published by the University Press

The Law of International Institutions in Europe
by A. H. Robertson, B.C.L., S.J.D., 1961
The Role of International Law in the Elimination of War
by Professor Quincy Wright, 1961
The Acquisition of Territory in International Law
by Professor R. Y. Jennings, 1962
The Sources and Evidences of International Law
by Clive Parry, LL.D., 1965
Rights in Air Space
by D. H. N. Johnson, M.A., LL.B., 1965
International Law and the Practitioner
by Sir Francis A. Vallat, K.C.M.G., Q.C., 1966
The Law of the Sea
by D. W. Bowett, M.A., LL.B., Ph.D., 1967
International Law and the Uses of Outer Space
by J. E. S. Fawcett, M.A., 1968
Modern Diplomatic Law
by M. Hardy, M.A., LL.M., 1968
The United Nations in a Changing World
by J. A. C. Gutteridge, M.A., 1970
Economic World Order?
by Professor Georg Schwarzenberger, 1970
An Introduction to the Law of the European Economic Community
edited by B. A. Wortley, O.B.E., Q.C., LL.D., 1972

OTHER BOOKS ON INTERNATIONAL LAW

Self-defence in International Law
by D. W. Bowett, M.A., LL.B., Ph.D.
Human Rights in Europe
by A. H. Robertson, B.C.L., S.J.D.
The Legal Problems of Foreign Investment in Developing Countries
by E. I. Nwogugu, LL.B., Ph.D.
Human Rights in National and International Law
edited by A. H. Robertson, B.C.L., S.J.D.
Legal Aspects of Foreign Investment in the European Economic Community
by W. H. Balekjian, Dr. rer. pol., Dr. Jur., Ph.D.
The Settlement of Boundary Disputes in International Law
by A. O. Cukwurah, B.C.L., LL.B., Ph.D.
East European Rules on the Validity of International Commercial Arbitration Agreements
by L. Kos-Rabcewicz-Zubkowski, LL.D.
Extradition in International Law
by I. A. Shearer, LL.M., S.J.D.
Human Rights in the World
by A. H. Robertson, B.C.L., S.J.D.
Privacy and Human Rights
edited by A. H. Robertson, B.C.L., S.J.D.

THE VIENNA CONVENTION ON THE LAW OF TREATIES

by

I. M. SINCLAIR, C.M.G.

SENIOR LEGAL ADVISOR
TO H.M. FOREIGN AND COMMONWEALTH OFFICE

MANCHESTER UNIVERSITY PRESS
U.S.A.: OCEANA PUBLICATIONS INC

Published by the University of Manchester at
THE UNIVERSITY PRESS
316–324 Oxford Road, Manchester M13 9NR
UK ISBN 0 7190 0541 8

USA and Canada
OCEANA PUBLICATIONS INC
75 Main Street, Dobbs Ferry, N.Y. 10522

Distributed in India by
N. M. TRIPATHI (PRIVATE) LTD
Princess Street, Bombay 2

Library of Congress Cataloguing-in-Publication Data

Sinclair, Ian McTaggart, 1926–

The Vienna convention on the law of treaties.

(The Melland Schill lectures)
Includes bibliographical references.
1. Vienna convention on the law of treaties.
I. Series.

JX4165.S55 341.3′7 72–13210
ISBN 0 7190 0541 8 (Manchester)
ISBN 0 379 11913 7 (Oceana)

Made and Printed in Great Britain by
Butler & Tanner Ltd, Frome and London

CONTENTS

FOREWORD

By her will the late Miss Olive Schill, of Prestbury, Cheshire, an old friend of the University, whose portrait is painted in Lady Katharine Chorley's *Manchester made them,* left the sum of £10,000 to the University in memory of her brother, Melland Schill, who died in the 1914–18 war. The annual income from this sum is to be used to promote and publish a series of public lectures, of the highest possible standard, dealing with international law.

Mr Sinclair writes about the Vienna Convention on the Law of Treaties from first-hand experience, because it was part of his professional duty as one of the Legal Advisers to the Foreign and Commonwealth Office to attend the conference in Vienna where the Convention was hammered out.

Clearly, the views are well-informed and learned. They are also, in my opinion, objective. They are, of course, the personal views of the author and do not have any official standing. The Schill lectures are academic exercises by competent international lawyers, but they do not aspire to express the views of any government.

I warmly commend this volume as putting in a relatively small compass the international law of treaties as reflected in the Vienna Convention. The volume will be of interest not only to Foreign Offices and embassies throughout the world but also to British practitioners who have to advise their own clients on the interpretation of treaties—a matter which is increasingly important since the country's entry into the Common Market.

My thanks are due to my friend Mr Reginald Pilkington, O.B.E., LL.M., for his invaluable assistance with the proofs, and to my son, Richard J. A. Wortley, LL.B., for preparing the list of articles of the Convention cited in the text, and also, as ever, to Mr T. L. Jones and his colleagues of the Press.

B. A. Wortley
Department of International Law
Faculty of Law
University of Manchester

CHAPTER I

THE SCOPE OF THE CONVENTION AND ITS RELATIONSHIP TO CUSTOMARY LAW

The Vienna Convention on the Law of Treaties was opened for signature at Vienna on 23 May 1969, following the successful conclusion of the United Nations Conference on the Law of Treaties which met at Vienna from 26 March to 24 May 1968, and from 9 April to 22 May 1969. The Convention is expressed to enter into force on the thirtieth day following the date of deposit of the thirty-fifth instrument of ratification or accession. Having regard to the significance of treaties as a primary source of international law, and having regard equally to the range and complexity of the law of treaties, it may be permissible to express satisfaction that this major enterprise in the field of codification and progressive development of international law—an enterprise which was embarked upon by the International Law Commission as early as 1949—has achieved finality. But satisfaction must be tempered with realism. The Convention is the product of many conflicting interests and viewpoints and has the customary vices of compromise. Among these is a tendency to overcome points of difficulty by expressing rules at a level of generality and abstraction sufficient to hide the underlying divergencies. This tendency is a feature of the drafting of the Convention to which we shall return in due course; for it is the purpose of these lectures to offer a critical analysis of the Convention against the background of pre-existing law and practice.

But before embarking on an analysis of the Convention I would like to say something about the broader perspective against which the Convention should be viewed. One has to seek to assess the significance of a Convention on the law of treaties in the light of certain traditional assumptions about the sources of international law in general. A previous lecturer in this series has undertaken a comprehensive and evocative survey of the sources of international law.[1] It is far from my purpose to cover the same ground as

[1] Parry, *The Sources and Evidences of International Law* (1965) in this Melland Schill Lecture series.

Professor Parry; nor indeed would I wish to do so. But still something remains to be said. Article 38 of the Statute of the International Court of Justice lists, among the matters which the Court is called upon to apply in order to decide in accordance with international law such disputes as are submitted to it, 'international Conventions, whether general or particular, establishing rules expressly recognised by the contracting States'. The fact that 'international Conventions' are listed first among the sources of international law on which the International Court can draw may imply a value judgment as to the place which treaties occupy in the hierarchy of sources, if such a hierarchy exists; on the other hand, it may simply be indicative of the logical concept that, the consent of States (whether express or tacit) being the method whereby rules of international law are effectively created or accorded recognition within the framework of an international society of individual nation States, one should first apply those rules to which assent has been specifically and expressly given before having recourse to rules (such as those deriving from international custom and general principles of law) whose validity depends more on the notion of tacit, rather than express, consent. As Lauterpacht puts it:

> The order in which the sources of international law are enumerated in the Statute of the International Court of Justice is, essentially, in accordance both with correct legal principle and with the character of international law as a body of rules based on consent to a degree higher than is law within the State. The rights and duties of States are determined, in the first instance, by their agreement as expressed in treaties—just as, in the case of individuals their rights are specifically determined by any contract which is binding upon them. When a controversy arises between two or more States with regard to a matter regulated by a treaty, it is natural that the parties should invoke and that the adjudicating agency should apply, in the first instance, the provisions of the treaty in question.[2]

So it would appear that, among the sources of international law, pride of place must be accorded to treaties precisely because they embody rules expressly recognised by the parties. But then, what is the source of the legal rules governing the conclusion, formation, interpretation and validity of treaties themselves? Prior to the conclusion of the Vienna Convention on the Law of Treaties, one

[2] Lauterpacht, *International Law: Collected Papers*, vol. 1, *General Works* (1970), p. 87.

would have asserted with a fair degree of confidence that the source (in the sense of that which gives to the content of rules of international law their character as law) of most of the rules of the law of treaties lay in international custom representing evidence of a general practice accepted as law. I deliberately refer to 'most' of the rules of the law of treaties, because I do not wish to venture into doctrinal arguments about the source (in the sense which I have used) of the most fundamental principle of treaty law—namely, *pacta sunt servanda*. That source is, and can only be, extra-legal in character. It is easy enough to posit the rule that every treaty in force is binding upon the parties to it; but the source of that rule rests, not on the principle of consent (which is, or may be, germane only as evidence that the rule is accepted as law), but rather on considerations relating to the binding force of international law in general, which of necessity leads us into somewhat metaphysical regions.[3]

But if the source of most of the rules of the law of treaties lay in international custom, what has been the effect of the conclusion of the Convention? Has it transformed pre-existing customary rules into conventional rules? Why, in any event, a treaty on the law of treaties? And what can be the source of validity of an international Convention on the law of treaties itself? Without seeking to engage in too rigorous or profound an analysis, I hope to show that these questions did not escape the attention of those responsible for the drafting of the Convention. To this end, I propose first to discuss why the codification of the law of treaties has itself been embodied in treaty form and then to consider, in somewhat greater detail, the relationship between the Vienna Convention and customary law.

WHY A TREATY ON THE LAW OF TREATIES?

The topic of the law of treaties was included in the work programme of the International Law Commission at its first session in 1949 and was placed high on the priority list of topics for codification. Progress in the early days was slow, partly because the Commission was heavily engaged on other matters. The first two Special Rapporteurs (the late Professors Brierly and Lauterpacht) appear to have pro-

[3] See Brierly, *The Basis of Obligation in International Law* (1958); and cf. Fitzmaurice, 'The foundations of the authority of international law and the problem of enforcement', *Modern Law Review* (1956), pp. 1–13.

ceeded on the assumption that the objective was to prepare draft articles which could form the basis of an eventual international Convention, although there was no specific decision by the Commission on this point.[4] However, when Sir Gerald Fitzmaurice was elected Special Rapporteur on the Law of Treaties in succession to Professor Lauterpacht in 1955 he raised, in his first report, the fundamental question of whether the codification of the law of treaties should take the form of an international Convention or of an expository code. Fitzmaurice himself favoured an expository code, for two principal reasons:

First, it seems inappropriate that a code on the law of treaties should itself take the form of a treaty; or rather, it seems more appropriate that it should have an independent basis. In the second place, much of the law relating to treaties is not especially suitable for framing in conventional form. It consists of enunciations of principles and abstract rules, most easily stated in the form of a code; and this also has the advantage of rendering permissible the inclusion of a certain amount of declaratory and explanatory material in the body of the code, in a way that would not be possible if this had to be confined to a strict statement of obligation.[5]

After a relatively brief debate at its eighth session in 1956, the Commission approved the proposal that codification of the law of treaties should take the form of an expository code. Doubts, however, appear to have arisen within the Commission when it was confronted with the five detailed reports submitted in successive years by Fitzmaurice. These incorporated, in the form of draft articles for a code, a considerable amount of descriptive material, based upon the author's long experience with treaty-making practice. The Commission was unable to devote much time to the five reports presented by Fitzmaurice before the latter resigned from the Commission following upon his election to the International Court of Justice in 1960 to fill the vacancy caused by the death of Judge Lauterpacht. However, in 1961 the Commission was obliged to reconsider the fundamental issue. Many members of the Commission, while paying tribute to the magisterial reports tabled by Fitzmaurice, expressed serious reservations about the basic approach. Those who, by virtue of their legal background and training, were more accustomed to a process of codification involving the establishment of general rules

[4] Rosenne, *The Law of Treaties: Guide to the Legislative History of the Vienna Convention* (1970), p. 34.

[5] *Yearbook of the International Law Commission* (1956), vol. II, p. 107.

of a normative character were particularly critical of the descriptive and analytical nature of the draft articles. Among the reasons advanced in favour of a Convention rather than a code were the following:

(*a*) that an expository code, however well formulated, could not, in the nature of things, be so effective as a Convention for consolidating the law; and
(*b*) that the codification of the law of treaties through a multilateral Convention would give all the new States the opportunity to participate directly in the formulation of the law if they so wished, which would be desirable in order to place the law of treaties upon the widest and most secure foundations.[6]

The Commission accordingly came to a clear decision in 1961 (and this decision was subsequently affirmed in 1962 and reaffirmed in 1965) that the codification of the law of treaties should be completed in a form which could serve as a basis for a Convention. It was subsequently disclosed that the new Special Rapporteur—Sir Humphrey Waldock—appointed to succeed Sir Gerald Fitzmaurice had virtually made his acceptance of the post conditional on the draft articles being given the form of a Convention.[7]

The hesitations of the Commission as to the precise form which the codification of the law of treaties should take were matched by similar hesitations on the part of certain governments. Although the vast majority of governments were generally in favour of formulating a Convention on the law of treaties on the basis of draft articles prepared by the Commission, some doubts remained, even as late as 1965. It was argued, for example, that 'consolidation' could be achieved just as well with a code as with a Convention, and that it was not essential to opt in favour of a Convention in order to secure the participation of the new States in the work of codification; it was also maintained that there was a certain logical inconsistency in drawing up a treaty on the method of drawing up a treaty, and that a treaty on treaties would inevitably create a dualistic system,

[6] *Yearbook of the International Law Commission* (1961), vol. II, p. 128.

[7] Statement by Professor Ago (chairman of the sixteenth session of the Commission) at the 851st meeting of the Sixth Committee of the General Assembly, held on 14 October 1965: G.A.O.R. (xx) A/C.6/SR 851; cf. also Rosenne, *op. cit.*, p. 34.

since it would apply between the parties to it, whereas the customary law would continue to apply as between other States.[8]

Despite the doctrinal doubts as to the value and usefulness of a treaty on treaties, the Commission, during the period between 1961 and 1966, sought to recast the material on which it was working into the form of draft articles suitable for incorporating into an international Convention. This involved discarding descriptive and exhortatory elements and producing a series of condensed texts confined to a statement of the legal principle or rule to be applied, qualified, as necessary, by a clause permitting the parties to any particular treaty to agree otherwise.[9]

So much for the reasons why the codification of the law of treaties has taken the form of an international Convention. But what, one may ask, is the consequence? What is the relationship between the Vienna Convention and customary international law?

RELATIONSHIP BETWEEN THE VIENNA CONVENTION AND CUSTOMARY INTERNATIONAL LAW

It is first necessary to say a few words about the scope of the Vienna Convention. A glance at the headings to the various Parts of the Convention quickly reveals that it covers all the topics traditionally regarded as falling within the framework of the law of treaties—that is to say, the conclusion and entry into force of treaties (including reservations), the observance, application and interpretation of treaties, the amendment and modification of treaties, and the invalidity, termination and suspension of operation of treaties. The Convention in addition lays down procedural rules concerning depositaries, notifications, corrections and registration. In sum, therefore, the Convention purports to constitute a comprehensive set of principles and rules governing all the most significant aspects of the law of treaties.

However, certain limitations should be noted at the outset. In the first place, the Convention is limited to treaties concluded between States (Article 1). Thus treaties concluded between States and international organisations, or between international organisations themselves, are deliberately excluded from the scope of the Convention.

[8] See statements by the representatives of Austria, France and Greece respectively at the 851st, 849th and 845th meetings of the Sixth Committee in 1965.

[9] Rosenne, *op. cit.*, pp. 35–8.

The Conference, however, recognising the importance of such treaties, adopted a resolution recommending that the General Assembly refer to the International Law Commission the study, in consultation with the principal international organisations, of the question of treaties concluded between States and international organisations or between two or more international organisations.[10] In the second place, the Convention is limited to international agreements concluded between States in written form and governed by international law, so that agreements *not* in written form, even if governed by international law, are not covered by the Convention.[11] In the third place, the Convention deliberately does not seek to regulate questions concerning succession to treaties, State responsibility and the effect of the outbreak of hostilities on treaties.[12] In the fourth place, the Convention is non-retroactive in its application—that is to say, it applies only to treaties which are concluded by States after the entry into force of the Convention with regard to such States.[13] Finally, many of the provisions of the Convention are expressed as residual rules which are to operate unless the treaty otherwise provides, or it is otherwise agreed by the parties, or a different intention is otherwise established. By means of this device, a considerable degree of liberty of action is left to the parties to any particular treaty; in large measure, the principle of the autonomy of the parties is preserved, and allowance is made for variations in treaty-making practice.

[10] Effect was given to this recommendation by operative para. 5 of General Assembly resolution 2501 (XXIV) of 12 November 1969. Subsequently the Commission established a sub-committee of thirteen members under the chairmanship of M. Reuter with the task of considering preliminary problems involved in the study of the new topic. On the basis of a report by the sub-committee, the Commission, at its 1078th meeting, held on 26 June 1970, requested the Secretary-General to prepare 'as soon as possible (preferably by 1 January 1971) a working paper on the subject, containing a short bibliography, a historical survey of the question and a preliminary list of the relevant treaties published in the United Nations Treaty Series': G.A.O.R. (XXV), Supplement No. 10 (A/8010), para. 89. Pursuant to this request, the Secretary-General submitted the working paper by the end of 1970: A/CN.4/L./161 and A/CN.4 L.161. Add. 1 of 28 December 1970 and 26 January 1971 respectively. At its 1971 session the Commission decided to appoint M. Reuter as Special Rapporteur on this topic.

[11] This results clearly from the terms of Articles 2(1)(a) (definition of the expression 'treaty') and 3 of the Convention.

[12] Article 73.

[13] Article 4.

Thus the Convention, although comprehensive in its scope, proves, on closer analysis, to be more restricted in its application than first appearances might suggest. This is self-evidently a factor to be taken into account in assessing the relationship between the Convention and customary international law.

That the authors of the Convention have been careful to preserve, where appropriate, the operation of rules of customary international law relating to treaties emerges from a study of the text. I propose to concentrate attention on four relevant provisions—Articles 3(b), 4, 38 and 43.

Article 3 of the Convention is concerned with international agreements not within the scope of the Convention—that is to say, international agreements concluded between States and other subjects of international law (for example, international organisations) and between such other subjects of international law, and international agreements not in written form. Sub-paragraph (b) of Article 3 declares that the rules set forth in the Convention to which such agreements 'would be subject under international law independently of the Convention' remain unaffected by the fact that the Convention does not in terms apply to them. At the first session of the Vienna conference several delegations expressed doubts as to the meaning of the phrase 'to which they would be subject independently of the Convention' (the language used by the Commission).[14] It was explained that the purpose of this phrase was to underline the concept that the rules set forth in the draft articles under discussion could be applied not only as conventional rules but also because they were rules of customary international law or general principles of law. The Drafting Committee, to which several amendments proposing the deletion or modification of this phrase had been transmitted, made only one minor change, inserting the phrase 'under international law' before 'independently of the Convention'. The chairman of the Drafting Committee explained that the phrase 'independently of the Convention' was necessary 'in order to show that the rules stated in the Convention could apply, not as articles of the Convention, but on other grounds, because they had another source; for example, custom'.[15]

[14] For example, the delegations of Switzerland, Gabon, Ethiopia, Mexico, Cuba, France and Greece.

[15] *United Nations Conference on the Law of Treaties, Official Records, First Session* (A/Conf. 39/11) (hereinafter cited as *Official Records, First Session*), 28th meeting (Yasseen).

Article 4 of the Convention establishes, as has already been noted, the general principle of non-retroactivity of the Convention. But this principle is again expressed as being 'without prejudice to the application of any rules set forth in the present Convention to which treaties would be subject under international law independently of the Convention'. It is perhaps of interest to spend a few moments analysing the debates at the Vienna conference on this most significant article. It did not appear in the final set of draft articles proposed by the Commission, although the principle of non-retroactivity of treaties in general was reflected in Article 24 of the draft articles proposed by the Commission.[16] A proposal specifically designed to make the Convention as such non-retroactive was first tabled by Venezuela late in the second session of the conference in 1969, when the conference began consideration of the final provisions of the Convention. The initial Venezuelan proposal was eventually withdrawn in favour of a five-power proposal introduced by the representative of Sweden. The five-power proposal preserved the operation of 'the rules of customary international law codified in the present Convention'. In introducing the proposal, the representative of Sweden stated:

> It was generally agreed that most of the contents of the present Convention were merely expressive of rules which existed under customary international law. Those rules obviously could be invoked as custom without any reference to the present Convention. But to the limited extent that the Convention laid down rules that were not rules of customary international law, those rules could not be so invoked. That position could be regarded as already made clear from the general rule contained in article 24[17] of the Convention. It might nevertheless be safer to make the point explicit in one of the final clauses.[18]

In subsequent debate it was pointed out that the five-power proposal was too restrictive in preserving only the operation of the rules of customary international law. It was necessary also to take into account general principles of law which were a separate source of international law. Furthermore, it was incorrect to restrict the

[16] *Reports of the International Law Commission on the Second Part of its Seventeenth Session and on its Eighteenth Session* (1966), G.A.O.R. (xxi) Supplement No. 9 (A/6309/Rev. 1), pp. 43–4 (hereinafter cited as '1966 I.L.C. Reports').

[17] Now Article 28.

[18] *Official Records, Second Session* (A/Conf. 39/11 Add. 1), 101st meeting (Committee of the Whole) (Blix).

operation of the rules of customary international law to those embodied in the present Convention; other rules of customary international law might be applicable. In deference to this criticism, the sponsors of the five-power proposal revised it to bring the wording more closely into line with that adopted for Article 3(b).

The third reference to customary international law is to be found in Article 38, which provides that nothing in Articles 34–37 (dealing with treaties and third States) 'precludes a rule set forth in a treaty from becoming binding upon a third State as a customary rule of international law, recognised as such'. Article 38 has its origin in Article 34 of the final set of draft articles on the law of treaties drawn up by the International Law Commission in 1966. In its commentary to Article 34 the Commission noted the role played by custom in sometimes extending the application of rules contained in a treaty beyond the contracting States. After citing the examples of treaties concluded between certain States which establish a territorial, fluvial or maritime regime and which afterwards come to be accepted by other States as binding upon them by way of custom, the Commission expressed the view that so also a 'codifying Convention purporting to state existing rules of customary international law may come to be regarded as the generally accepted formulation of the customary rules in question even by States not parties to the Convention'.[19] But, the Commission went on, these were not cases of the treaty itself having legal effects for third States. For the third States concerned, the source of the binding force of rules formulated in a treaty to which they are not parties is custom, not the treaty.

At the conference there was a certain amount of criticism of this particular draft article. It was not disputed that there did exist a process whereby rules contained in a treaty might become binding on third States as rules of customary international law. But it was maintained that this process had nothing to do with the law of treaties. How treaty rules become transformed into customary rules was part and parcel of the principles governing the growth and formation of custom. Despite this cogent line of argument, the majority of delegations represented at the conference favoured the retention of a provision on the lines of Article 34 of the I.L.C. draft, if only, as Sir Humphrey Waldock pointed out, to 'obviate any

[19] 1966 I.L.C. Reports, p. 61.

misunderstanding' about the legal effects of the preceding series of articles on treaties and third States.[20]

Article 43 of the Convention establishes the general principle that the invalidity, termination or denunciation of a treaty, the withdrawal of a party from it, or the suspension of its operation, as a result of the application of the Convention or of the provisions of the treaty, does not in any way impair the duty of any State to fulfil any obligation embodied in the treaty to which it would be subject under international law independently of the treaty. In commenting on the draft of this provision at the first session of the conference, the United States representative, Mr Briggs (at that time a member of the International Law Commission) stated that 'it contained a very important rule of international law that complemented the provision of Article [38] under which a rule set forth in a treaty might become binding upon a third State as a customary rule of international law'.

I have discussed the four provisions of the Convention itself which are directly relevant to this question of the relationship between the Convention and customary international law. But it would be wrong of me to conclude on this aspect without making mention of the preamble to the Convention. The final clause of the preamble to the Convention, following, in this respect, the precedents afforded by the preambles to the Vienna Convention on Diplomatic Relations and the Vienna Convention on Consular Relations, affirms that 'the rules of international customary law will continue to govern questions not regulated by the provisions of the present Convention'. This preambular clause does not, of course, have a direct bearing on the relationship between the rules laid down in the Convention and existing rules of customary international law. It is intended simply as a saving for those rules of customary international law relating to the law of treaties which govern questions not regulated by the Convention. In the words of the Swiss sponsor of the proposal to add to the preamble a clause of this nature, 'the conference had succeeded in reducing a new and substantial part of customary law to writing; but gaps remained, so that occasionally it was still necessary, in the practice of international relations, to fall back on custom'.[21]

[20] *Official Records, First Session,* 36th meeting.

[21] *Official Records, Second Session,* 31st plenary meeting (Ruegger).

THE CONVENTION RULES: CODIFICATION OR PROGRESSIVE DEVELOPMENT?

So far, we have established that the drafters of the Convention were aware of the complex interrelationship between the rules embodied in the Convention and the existing rules of customary international law. They did not seek to define this interrelationship further than to preserve, where appropriate, the applicability of any rules contained in the Convention to which treaties would be subject under international law independently of the Convention. Is it possible to distinguish between those provisions of the Convention which simply formulate existing rules of customary, or general, international law and those provisions which involve an extension or development of the existing rules? This requires an analysis of the distinction between codification and progressive development.

Article 15 of the Statute of the International Law Commission defines the expression 'progressive development of international law' for the purposes of the Statute as meaning 'the preparation of draft Conventions on subjects which have not yet been regulated by international law or in regard to which the law has not yet been sufficiently developed in the practice of States'. Similarly, it defines the expression 'codification of international law' as meaning 'the more precise formulation and systemisation of rules of international law in fields where there already has been extensive State practice, precedent and doctrine'.

This distinction between the two concepts has proved extremely difficult for the Commission to sustain in practice. Originally, the distinction was considered to be of great importance so far as the methods and procedures of the Commission were concerned. Doubt had been expressed as to the desirability of using the Convention method for codification in the narrow sense. It was pointed out in particular, in a memorandum prepared by the United Nations Secretariat in 1947, that the failure of governments to reach agreement, for political reasons, in a conference convened to codify rules of international law would seem to cast doubt on certain rules of international law whose validity had been admitted for a very long time and which had hitherto generally been assumed to be part of customary international law.[22] For this and other reasons it was

[22] 'Memorandum on Methods for Encouraging the Progressive Development of International Law and its Eventual Codification', A/AC.10/7 of 6 May 1947, p. 7.

felt that there might be utility in the preparation of scientific restatements of existing international law by an impartial group of jurists, possibly as a preliminary step to prepare the ground for eventual codification by international agreement.[23]

But the experience of the International Law Commission has proved that a clear and sharp dividing line between codification and progressive development is, in any particular case, impossible to establish. When submitting, in 1953, its draft Convention on Arbitral Procedure, the Commission pointed out that the draft fell within the categories both of progressive development of international law and the codification of international law. In 1956 the Commission submitted to the General Assembly a final set of draft articles on the law of the sea. In its report covering these draft articles the Commission stated:

> In preparing its rules on the law of the sea, the Commission has become convinced that, in this domain at any rate, the distinction established in the Statute between these two activities [i.e. progressive development and codification] can hardly be maintained. Not only may there be wide differences of opinion as to whether a subject is already 'sufficiently developed in practice', but also several of the provisions adopted by the Commission, based on a 'recognised principle of international law' have been framed in such a way as to place them in the 'progressive development' category. Although it tried at first to specify which articles fell into one and which into the other category, the Commission has had to abandon the attempt, as several do not wholly belong to either.[24]

Thus it will be seen that, from a very early stage, the Commission had encountered difficulty in distinguishing clearly between the progressive development of international law and its codification. It is clear that the very act of formulating a rule which is generally thought to reflect State practice, precedent and doctrine may involve the transformation of that rule into progressive development, for example, where it is found necessary or desirable to incorporate

[23] *Loc. cit.*, p. 8; see also Briggs, *The International Law Commission* (1965), pp. 129–41.

[24] *Report of the International Law Commission covering the work of its Eighth Session* (1956), G.A.O.R. (XI), Supplement No. 9 (A/3159), para. 26; for a fuller survey of the distinction between codification and progressive development see Dhokalia, *The Codification of Public International Law* (1970), pp. 203–16.

a qualification or exception in relation to which the practice of States is ambivalent or conflicting.

The Commission, in submitting its final set of draft articles on the law of treaties, followed previous practice in refusing to categorise its work starkly as either progressive development or codification. In its covering report the Commission stated:

> The Commission's work on the law of treaties constitutes both codification and progressive development of international law in the sense in which those concepts are defined in Article 15 of the Commission's Statute, and, as was the case with several previous drafts, it is not practicable to determine into which category each provision falls. Some of the commentaries, however, indicate that certain new rules are being proposed for the consideration of the General Assembly and of Governments.[25]

It might be thought that the clue suggested in the last sentence of the passage just cited would enable one to identify clearly those rules proposed by the Commission which were considered to involve progressive development rather than codification. But a careful scrutiny of the commentaries dispels this illusion. It is only in rare cases, and then by implication rather than by express pronouncement, that one can determine where the Commission has put forward a proposal by way of progressive development rather than by way of codification.

The first provision in the Convention which clearly seems to involve progressive development rather than codification is Article 9(2), which provides that the adoption of the text of a treaty at an international conference takes place by the vote of two-thirds of the States present and voting, unless by the same majority they decide to apply a different rule. In its commentary to the proposal on which this provision is based, the Commission states that 'in former times the adoption of the text of a treaty almost always took place by the agreement of all the States participating in the negotiations and unanimity could be said to be the general rule'. But, went on the Commission, the growth of the practice of drawing up treaties in large international conferences or within international organisations had led to so normal a use of the procedure of majority vote that, in its opinion, 'it would be *unrealistic*' to lay down unanimity as the general rule for the adoption of the texts of treaties drawn up

[25] 1966 I.L.C. Reports, p. 10.

at conferences or within organisations.[26] In the course of debate at the first session, Mr Yasseen (Iraq), a member of the International Law Commission, stated unequivocally that 'paragraph 2 contained a rule which represented progressive development of international law and was based on international practice'.[27]

A further example of where a proposal by the Commission represented progressive development rather than codification is afforded by the text of Article 15(a) of the final set of draft articles adopted by the Commission in 1966. This particular proposal stipulated that 'a State is obliged to refrain from acts tending to frustrate the object of a proposed treaty when . . . it has agreed to enter into negotiations for the conclusion of the treaty, while those negotiations are in progress'. At the first session of the conference this proposal was harshly criticised. In the view of the Venezuelan representative, sub-paragraph (a) 'laid down a new principle of international law'. The Swiss representative asserted that the rule 'was new and seemed to go beyond the scope of codification'. To the Greek representative the rule in sub-paragraph (a) 'might be termed a sweeping development of international law', while to the Indian representative the rule 'was a new one and did not derive from doctrine, case law or practice'. The Austrian representative considered that sub-paragraph (a) 'went far beyond existing rules of international law' and the German delegate maintained that it 'had no support in international law or practice and was hardly advisable from the point of view of progressive development of international law'.[28] Replying to the debate, Sir Humphrey Waldock (who acted as Expert Consultant to the Conference) conceded that, in putting forward this proposal:

the Commission had not based itself on any specific authority or precedent, and would not wish to maintain that the principle stated in Article 15 sub-paragraph (a) was a rule of customary international law. Whether its proposal should be regarded as progressive development or as codification of the law was a matter of opinion.[29]

[26] 1966 I.L.C. Reports, p. 27.

[27] *Official Records, First Session*, 15th meeting. See also the statement by Mr Ruda (Argentina), also a member of the Commission, at the same meeting. Ruda maintained that 'the provisions of paragraph 2, on the other hand, did not constitute a rule of positive international law'; they represented 'progressive development'.

[28] These statements can be found in *Official Records, First Session*, 19th meeting.

[29] *Official Records, First Session*, 20th meeting.

In the event, sub-paragraph (a) was deleted by decision of the conference, and the remainder of what was Article 15 in the I.L.C. draft now appears, with a number of drafting modifications, as Article 18 of the Convention.

It can also be said, with a fair degree of confidence, that the series of articles on reservations (Articles 19–23 of the Convention) represent, at least in some measure, progressive development rather than codification. The commentary to the draft articles prepared by the Commission sets out in some detail the complex history of developments concerning reservations to multilateral Conventions. There is no doubt that the advisory opinion given by the International Court in 1951 in the case concerning 'Reservations to the Genocide Convention'[30] had brought about a movement away from the traditional unanimity rule whereby a reservation, in order to be valid, must have the assent of all interested States. On the other hand, those who adhered to the extreme 'sovereignty' school of thought, according to which every State has an absolute sovereign right to make reservations at will and to become a party to international Conventions subject to such reservations, and notwithstanding any objection made to them, were not satisfied with the limited move away from the unanimity rule represented by the principle underlying the 'Genocide Convention' case. There was no doubt that the subject of reservations to multilateral Conventions was one where the pre-Convention state of the law was uncertain and controversial, and where differing theories were held with conviction. The flexible Convention regime on reservations (about which more will be said at a later stage) is based, in large measure, on the pan-American system, but it would be a bold jurist who would assert, with any degree of confidence, that the Convention regime represents in its entirety codification rather than rules of progressive development.

It seems clear that certain of the rules set out in Articles 40 and 41 of the Convention, relating respectively to the amendment and the *inter se* modification of multilateral treaties, constitute progressive development rather than codification. McNair points out that 'as a matter of principle, no State has a legal right to demand the revision of a treaty in the absence of some provision to that effect contained in that treaty or in some other treaty to which it is a party' and that 'treaty revision is a matter for politics and

[30] *I.C.J. Reports* (1951), p. 15.

diplomacy and has little, if any, place in this book'.[31] It has none the less become customary to incorporate in recent multilateral Conventions specific provisions as to the means by which the amendment of the Convention may be affected. The Commission, however, proposed that a distinction should be drawn between amendment and *inter se* modification and that residual rules should be established to deal with the case where a treaty is silent on the question of revision. The conference accepted the substance of the proposals advanced by the Commission, although at least one delegation commented that the text of what is now Article 40 'represented the progressive development of international law and might give rise to some practical difficulties', and the Expert Consultant, Sir Humphrey Waldock, stated, with reference to paragraph 5 of Article 40, that it involved 'a presumption . . . *de lege ferenda* of the intention (of the State concerned) to become a party to the amended version of the treaty'.[32]

Much more controversial is the question of how far the rules relating to the invalidity, termination and suspension of the operation of treaties set out in Part V of the Convention represent progressive development rather than codification *stricto sensu*. This applies in particular to such grounds of invalidity as error, fraud, corruption, coercion of a representative of a State, coercion of a State by the threat or use of force or conflict with a peremptory norm of general international law (*jus cogens*) as set out in Articles 48–53 of the Convention. A fuller analysis of these controversial grounds of invalidity will be given at a later stage. At this point, it is proposed simply to concentrate on the issue whether these grounds of invalidity constitute progressive development rather than codification, and to take as a basis for the discussion the I.L.C. commentaries and the records of the conference.

As regards error, the Commission, in their commentary to the relevant provisions in the final set of draft articles, concede that 'the instances in which errors of substance have been invoked as affecting the essential validity of a treaty have not been frequent' and that 'almost all the recorded instances concern geographical errors, and most of them concern errors in maps'.[33] The two cases

[31] *Law of Treaties* (1961), p. 534.

[32] *Official Records, First Session*, 36th and 37th meetings.

[33] 1966 I.L.C. Reports, p. 72; cf. Cukwurah, *The Settlement of Boundary Disputes in International Law* (1967), p. 181.

cited by the Commission (the 'Eastern Greenland' case[34] and the 'Temple' case[35]) throw light only on the conditions under which error will *not* vitiate consent rather than on those under which it will do so, as the Commission itself admitted. Against this background, there is (or may be) a question as to how far Article 48 of the Convention represents progressive development rather than codification. Certainly, paragraph 1 of Article 48 confines the right of States to invoke error within quite narrow limits and could be said to derive from *dicta* in the 'Temple' case. But the question was raised at the conference whether the article covers all possible instances of error—for example, error brought about by innocent misrepresentation. Furthermore, it was pointed out that paragraph 2 was incomplete in that it omitted the defence that the party advancing the error could have avoided it by the exercise of reasonable diligence. It will be recalled that, in the 'Temple' case, the International Court had stated:

> It is an established rule of law that the plea of error cannot be allowed as an element vitiating consent, if the party advancing it contributed by its own conduct to the error, *or could have avoided it*, or if the circumstances were such as to put that party on notice of a possible error.[36]

An amendment proposed by the United States delegation sought to reintroduce the missing phrase, but the amendment was rejected on a vote at the first session of the conference.

To sum up on this point, it would seem that there is a certain amount of jurisprudence on the effect of error in a treaty, but that Article 48 of the Convention involves some measure of progressive development as well as of codification.

Examples of fraud are rare, if not non-existent, in treaty law. The Commission were unable to cite any instances and admitted that 'in international law, the paucity of precedents means that there is little guidance to be found either in practice or in the jurisprudence of international tribunals as to the scope to be given to the concept'.[37] No definition was attempted by the Commission of the term 'fraudulent conduct' which it incorporated into the text

[34] P.C.I.J. (1933), Series A/B, No. 53, p. 71.
[35] *I.C.J. Reports* (1961), p. 30.
[36] *I.C.J. Reports* (1962), p. 26.
[37] 1966 I.L.C. Reports, p. 73.

of its proposal; but the Commission indicated that the expression was 'designed to include any false statements, misrepresentations or other deceitful proceedings by which a State is induced to give a consent to a treaty which it would not otherwise have given'. The Commission also sounded a warning against seeking to apply to the interpretation of the concept in international law the detailed connotations given to such expressions as 'fraud' or '*dol*' in international law.

The vagueness and uncertain effect of the Commission's proposal on fraud led to an attempt at the first session of the conference to secure the deletion of this article; but it was retained in the text by a large majority. Although it would no doubt be right to characterise fraud as a general principle of law which operates to vitiate consent, the application of this concept to the law of treaties does not derive much, if any, support from State practice and precedent. Accordingly, Article 48 must be accounted to involve some measure of progressive development.

An even more striking example of progressive development is Article 50, which permits a State to invoke the corruption of its representative as a ground for invalidating its consent to be bound by a treaty. The Commission had not included any specific rule on corruption in the set of draft articles which it had provisionally adopted in 1963, and it was indeed only at its final session, in 1966, that the proposal which forms the basis for Article 50 of the Convention was adopted by the Commission. The Commission was unable to cite any example in State practice of a treaty having been procured through the corruption of the representative of a State. To a number of delegations represented at the conference, corruption was only another form of fraud and should not be included as a separate ground of invalidity.[38] To others, such as the representative of Greece, Article 50 'boldly inaugurated a new institution of international law'.[39]

Article 51 of the Convention provides that the expression of a State's consent to be bound by a treaty which has been procured by the coercion of its representative through acts or threats directed against him shall be without any legal effect. This accordingly

[38] *Official Records, First Session,* 46th and 47th meetings (Mexico, Chile, Switzerland, Japan and United Kingdom).

[39] *Ibid.*

appears to be a case of absolute nullity. McNair appears to take the view that coercion directed against the representatives of a State may invalidate consent; but he argues that, if the treaty requires ratification and has been freely and knowingly ratified by the appropriate organ of the State, that ratification should wipe out the effect of any threat or application of force to the person signing the treaty.[40]

The notion that coercion directed against the representative of a State may be invoked by the State concerned as a ground for invalidating its consent to be bound by the treaty has a basis in customary international law; what is new in the formulation of Article 51 is the concept of absolute, rather than relative, nullity.

Article 52 of the Convention deals with coercion of the State itself and lays down a rule of absolute nullity. The Commission, after reviewing the history of the matter and taking into account the clear-cut prohibition of the threat or use of force in Article 2(4) of the United Nations Charter, considered that these developments 'justify the conclusion that the invalidity of a treaty procured by the illegal threat or use of force is a principle which is *lex lata* in the international law of today'.[41] Discussion at the conference on this article tended to concentrate on two issues:

(*a*) Whether the expression 'threat or use of force' could, or should, be interpreted as covering economic and political pressure.

(*b*) The temporal application of the rule—that is to say, the date from which the rule invalidating a treaty procured by the threat or use of force in violation of the principles of international law embodied in the Charter may be said to operate.

The records of the conference reveal strongly conflicting views on both these points.[42] That the rule now embodied in Article 52 of the Convention represents the modern law on this topic is beyond serious dispute; but there are clearly uncertainties about the

[40] *Op. cit.*, pp. 207–8.

[41] 1966 I.L.C. Reports, p. 75.

[42] As to the first point, see Kearney and Dalton, 'The treaty on treaties', 64 *A.J.I.L.* (1970), pp. 532–5; as to the second, see Jacobs, 'Innovation and continuity in the law of treaties', *Modern Law Review* 33 (1970), pp. 514–5.

scope of the rule and its temporal application, and these uncertainties are not removed by the lapidary formulation of the article.

Finally, we come to *jus cogens*. The concept that a treaty is void if, at the time of its conclusion, it conflicts with a peremptory norm of general international law must be regarded as the most significant instance of progressive development in the Convention as a whole. Some, of course, would deny this. Nahlik, for example, claims that 'the provision of the Vienna Convention declaring void treaties which are contrary to a norm of international *jus cogens* is not an invention of either the International Law Commission or the Vienna conference' but is based on the concept that 'the freedom of States in concluding treaties had *already* been restricted by the progressive development of international law'.[43] But the controversy surrounding the existence even of rules of *jus cogens*, far less their definition and identification, requires one to analyse the issue closely. Schwarzenberger's stark and uncompromising statement that 'international law on the level of unorganised international society does not know of any *jus cogens*'[44] may perhaps be over-bold; but it is striking that a concept so widely supported in doctrine and in the writings of jurists[45] has found so little application in State practice. It may be conceded that any developed system of law must dispose of certain rules of a higher order than those of a merely dispositive character from which persons subject to the law are free to contract out. It may also be conceded that there is a general recognition that there exist certain fundamental rules of international law, such as the rule prohibiting the threat or use of force in international relations, from which States cannot derogate by treaty. But the definition and identification of these rules of the 'higher law' is surrounded by immense difficulties. The Commission itself admitted that 'there is no simple criterion by which to identify a general rule of international law as having the character of *jus cogens*'.[46] The records of the conference reveal a wide variety of opinions as to the scope and content of *jus cogens*. This lack of agreement on the

[43] Nahlik, 'The grounds of invalidity and termination of treaties', 65 A.J.I.L. (1971), p. 745.

[44] 'International *jus cogens*', first published in *Texas Law Review* (1965) and reprinted in *The Concept of Jus Cogens in International Law* (1967), p. 138.

[45] For an analysis of the history of the concept, see Suy in *The Concept of Jus Cogens in International Law* (1967), pp. 18–76.

[46] 1966 I.L.C. Reports, p. 76.

essential content of *jus cogens* is in itself sufficient evidence that the rule embodied in Article 53 of the Convention bears the hallmark of progressive development rather than codification.

It may be noted that, referring to the series of articles on error, fraud, corruption and so on, Sir Francis Vallat had this to say on behalf of the United Kingdom delegation at the second session of the conference:

It had often been stated that many, if not all, of the articles merely put into writing existing principles or rules of international law, but his delegation very much doubted whether that was altogether true. Whether it was true or not, the articles undoubtedly contained a substantial element of progressive development, if only as regards their formulation and modalities and the procedures for their application. By any normal, legislative standards, the articles as drafted were in many respects broad and vague; such key words as 'fraud' and 'coercion', difficult enough to interpret in municipal law, and not previously applied in international law, were left completely undefined.[47]

Before concluding on this aspect, it may be useful to consider the views expressed by other commentators on the extent to which the rules embodied in the Convention constitute progressive development or codification. Nisot, in a trenchant contribution, argues that Article 18 of the Convention concerning the obligation not to defeat the object and purpose of a treaty prior to its entry into force constitutes a new regime which amounts to a derogation from customary international law.[48] O'Connell likewise takes the view that Article 18 of the Vienna Convention 'goes further than customary international law would appear to go.' He argues that the provision is at once more rigid and more relaxed than the principle of good faith on which it is said to be based—more rigid in the sense that it omits the relevance of circumstances and more relaxed in that it relates the obligation only to the 'object and purpose' of the treaty, and not to its incidents.[49]

It has also been argued that Article 46 of the Convention is to some extent innovative in restricting the right to invoke a violation of constitutional law as a ground for invalidating the consent of a State to be bound by a treaty.[50] This is debatable ground, since much

[47] *Official Records, Second Session,* 18th plenary meeting.

[48] *Revue Belge de Droit International* (1970–1), p. 501.

[49] *International Law,* second edition, vol. 1 (1970), pp. 223–4.

[50] Jacobs, *loc. cit.*, pp. 510–12.

depends on whether one starts from the position that constitutional limitations on the treaty-making power are, as it were, incorporated into international law so as to render voidable any consent to a treaty given on the international plane in violation of a constitutional limitation; or from the position that international law leaves to each State the determination of the organs and procedures by which its will to conclude treaties is formed, and is itself concerned exclusively with the external manifestations of this will on the international plane (subject perhaps to a qualification in cases where a State is aware, or must be assumed to be aware, of a lack of constitutional authority on the part of another negotiating State). As the weight of international jurisprudence and State practice has in recent years tended to favour the second or 'internationalist' position,[51] it may be doubted whether Article 46 of the Convention involves any material element of progressive development.

This brief analysis of the extent to which some of the more significant provisions of the Convention can be said to represent, at least in part, progressive development rather than codification is not intended to be exhaustive. It is rather intended to illustrate the thesis that the distinction between progressive development and codification becomes increasingly blurred when the attempt is made to spell out in conventional form rules deriving their source from international custom or from general principles of law. The distinction nevertheless remains one of prime importance to the practitioner as well as to the theorist. The question is: to what extent will the rules embodied in the Convention bind States not parties to the Convention as well as States parties to it? We have hitherto considered the extent to which the provisions of the Convention represent progressive development rather than codification. It now remains to investigate whether, and if so to what extent, the Convention itself may *generate* rules which will be accepted and recognised as customary rules of international law, notwithstanding that they do not have all the characteristics of such customary rules.

TREATY AND CUSTOM: RELEVANCE OF THE 'NORTH SEA CONTINENTAL SHELF' CASE

The process by which rules embodied in a multilateral Convention may come to be recognised and accepted as rules of customary or

[51] 1966 I.L.C. Reports, pp. 70–1.

general international law to which States are subject independently of the Convention has been described in the following terms by the International Court of Justice in the 'North Sea continental shelf' case:

The Court must now proceed to the last stage in the argument put forward on behalf of Denmark and the Netherlands. This is to the effect that even if there was at the date of the Geneva Convention no rule of customary international law in favour of the equidistance principle and no such rule was crystallised in Article 6 of the Convention, nevertheless such a rule has come into being since the Convention, partly because of its own impact, partly on the basis of subsequent State practice—and that this rule, being now a rule of customary international law binding on all States, including therefore the Federal Republic, should be declared applicable to the delimitation of the boundaries between the Parties' respective continental shelf areas in the North Sea.

In so far as this contention is based on the view that Article 6 of the Convention has had the influence, and has produced the effect, described, it clearly involves treating that Article as a norm-creating provision which has generated a rule which, while only conventional or contractual in its origin, has since passed into the general *corpus* of international law, and is now accepted as such by the *opinio juris*, so as to have become binding even for countries which have never, and do not, become parties to the Convention. There is no doubt that this process is a perfectly possible one and does from time to time occur: it constitutes indeed one of the recognised methods by which new rules of customary international law may be formed. At the same time, this result is not lightly to be regarded as having been attained.[52]

The Court, having accorded a cautious recognition to the process whereby certain multilateral Conventions may generate rules which gradually come to be accepted as forming part of customary international law, immediately proceeded to indicate, in general terms, the conditions which must be satisfied before the process can be regarded as having been effective. In the first place, the conventional provision whose transformation into a rule of customary rule is in question must 'be of a fundamentally norm-creating character such as could be regarded as forming the basis of a general rule of law'. In the second place there must be a very widespread and representative participation in the Convention, particularly of those States whose interests are specifically affected. In the third place,

[52] *I.C.J. Reports* (1969), p. 41.

there must be the *opinion juris* reflected in an extensive State practice virtually uniform in the sense of the provision invoked. The Court appears to discount the importance of the time element, treating this as being subsidiary to the requirement of the *opinio juris*.

Applying these conditions to the circumstances of the particular case, the Court concluded 'that if the Geneva Convention was not in its origins or inception declaratory of a mandatory rule of customary international law enjoining the use of the equidistance principle for the delimitation of continental shelf areas between adjacent States, neither has its subsequent effect been constitutive of such a rule; and that State practice up to date has equally been insufficient for the purpose'.[53]

What conclusion can we draw from the judgment of the Court in the 'North Sea continental shelf' case? First, and perhaps most important, the Court has in terms recognised the possibility that customary international law may be generated by treaty. But it has carefully qualified this recognition by establishing a series of conditions which, in the instant case, it was found had not been fulfilled. The caution displayed by the Court hardly justifies the conclusion that it was seeking to establish a new doctrine or methodological rule of looking to the manifest intent of the treaty itself in determining whether any provision in the treaty generates customary international law.[54] True it is that the Court analysed in detail the drafting history of Article 6(2) of the Continental Shelf Convention and the relationship between this and other provisions of the Convention. It attached importance to the fact that Article 6(2) of the Convention imposed a primary obligation to effect delimitation by agreement, putting second the obligation to make use of the equidistance method; this, the Court maintained, constitutes an unusual preface to what was claimed to be a potential general rule of law. The notion of 'special circumstances' embodied in Article 6 of the Convention raised further doubts as to the potentially norm-creating character of the equidistance principle. Finally, the fact that Article 12 of the Convention permitted reservations to be made to Article 6 was regarded as adding to the difficulty of considering Article 6 to be capable of generating a rule of customary international law. But the Court did not simply deduce the non-

[53] *Loc. cit.*, p. 45.

[54] D'Amato, 'Manifest intent and the generation by treaty of customary rules of international law', 64 *A.J.I.L.* (1970), pp. 892–902.

generating effect of Article 6 from the terms of the Convention itself; it devoted considerable space to establishing that State practice in the sense of the provision involved was neither as extensive nor as uniform as had been claimed, but that, even if it were, it would still be insufficient unless the State activity was motivated by the 'belief that this practice is rendered obligatory by the existence of a rule of law requiring it'.[55] It may be that, as Baxter claims, this requirement is unduly severe, and that *opinio juris* should be considered as being presumptively present unless evidence can be adduced that a State was acting from other than a sense of legal obligation.[56] The fact nonetheless remains that the judgment suggests clearly defined limits to the process of generation by treaty of customary rules, and that these limits involve the consideration of criteria external to the treaty itself.

To sum up, it may be said that the Vienna Convention on the Law of Treaties is in part declaratory of existing customary law, and in part a deliberate exercise in progressive development. To what extent those provisions of the Convention which recognisably constitute progressive development may come in time to generate rules of customary international law will depend on a number of elements which are at present unknown—the extent of participation in the Convention, the development of State practice and, above all, the interaction between norm-creating and procedural provisions. This last is a factor which is perhaps unique to the Vienna Convention on the Law of Treaties; but the drafting history of the Convention makes it abundantly clear that, for the majority of States, the acceptance of certain norm-creating provisions, particularly in Part V of the Convention, was conditional upon the inclusion in the Convention of specific procedural safeguards. It may therefore be concluded that this special feature of the Vienna Convention will constitute an additional hurdle to be overcome in seeking to establish, in the future, the custom-generating effect of particular Convention rules.

[55] *I.C.J. Reports* (1969), p. 44.
[56] Baxter, 'Treaties and custom', *Recueil des Cours* 129 (1970) p. 69.

CHAPTER II

THE CONCLUSION AND ENTRY INTO FORCE OF TREATIES

Part III of the Vienna Convention deals with the conclusion and entry into force of treaties. It is divided into three sections, the first relating to the conclusion of treaties (Articles 6–18), the second to reservations (Articles 19–23) and the third to entry into force and provisional application (Articles 24 and 25). I propose to take these three sections in order and to concentrate attention on the more important doctrinal and practical issues involved.

I CONCLUSION OF TREATIES

The series of articles relating to the conclusion of treaties follows a certain logical pattern, a pattern dictated by the order in time at which the various acts involved in the treaty-making process are executed. First, certain rules are established as to the authority of diplomatic or other agents of the State to negotiate and subsequently to adopt or authenticate the text of a treaty; those rules naturally embrace the circumstances in which full powers are required. The second stage is, of course, the stage of negotiation itself, and here the Convention contains provisions relating to the adoption and authentication of the text of a treaty. Next in order comes the means whereby States express their consent to be bound by a treaty, namely, signature, exchange of instruments, ratification, acceptance, approval or accession. Finally, there is the period, if any, between signature of a treaty and its entry into force; here the Convention lays down a rule, which we have already considered briefly, relating to the obligation of a State which has signed a treaty, or otherwise expressed its consent to be bound by it, not to defeat the object and purpose of that treaty prior to its entry into force.

I FULL POWERS

The first stage in the treaty-making process is to establish the authority of the representatives of the negotiating State or States concerned to perform the necessary formal acts involved in the drawing up of the text of a treaty or in the conclusion of a treaty. This authority is in principle determined by the issuance of a formal document entitled a 'full power' which designates a named individual or individuals to represent the State for the purpose of negotiating and concluding a treaty. Historically, the full power was of much greater significance than it is today. The original purpose of a full power, during the period of absolute monarchy, when treaties were contracted in form and in substance in the name of and as an expression of the will of the sovereign, was to clothe the personal agent of the sovereign with power to bind his principal, provided that he acted within the limits of his authority.[1] It was thus of fundamental importance that the authority of the agent should be defined with precision in advance of the negotiation, and considerable emphasis was placed on the form of the instrument, the more particularly as, depending on the language used, a refusal on the part of the sovereign to ratify the treaty concluded by his agent could be justified only on the basis that the agent had exceeded his authority.[2] Thus it is not surprising that the early history of full powers is replete with examples of lengthy and meticulous discussion of the meaning and significance to be attached to the particular phraseology employed in full powers.

Two related developments led to a decline in the importance attached to full powers. The first was the end of the period of absolute monarchy, which, for present purposes, can be fixed towards the conclusion of the eighteenth century. With the gradual establishment of a measure of diplomatic control over foreign policy following upon the American and French revolutions, it came to be accepted in State practice that ratification was discretionary, even if the agent who had negotiated the treaty had acted within the limits of the authority confided to him by the full power. The second was the increasing ease of communications, culminating in the development of the electric telegraph, which rendered it possible for negotiators to ensure that they were not exceeding the limits of their authority.

In more modern times a third factor has been at work which has accentuated the decline in the significance of full powers. This is the increasing tendency of States to conclude agreements in simplified form, that is to say, by exchange of notes or exchange of letters, there-

[1] McNair, *op. cit.*, p. 120.

[2] O'Connell, *op. cit.*, p. 211.

by dispensing with the need to produce full powers. This more informal approach to the conclusion of treaties is no doubt attributable to the increasing complexity of international relations, requiring a much wider and more comprehensive nexus of treaty links than was thought necessary in the earlier part of this century. International co-operation in such technical fields as telecommunications, the safety of life at sea, the protection of industrial property, air services and sanitary regulations has resulted in the construction of whole networks of treaty relationships which were undreamt of a hundred years ago. The rapid expansion of the international community with the advent of new States in Africa and Asia has meant a corresponding increase in the range of treaty links. It is accordingly not surprising that all these developments, requiring, as they do, a streamlining of the treaty-making process, have been accompanied by a tendency to simplify the formalities involved in the conclusion of treaties.

Article 7 of the Vienna Convention reflects these disparate, but parallel, tendencies. It first of all sets out the general rule that a person is considered as representing a State for the purpose of adopting or authenticating the text of a treaty or for the purpose of expressing the consent of the State to be bound by a treaty if:

(*a*) he produces full powers; or

(*b*) it appears from the practice of the States concerned or from other circumstances that their intention was to consider that person as representing the State for such purposes and to dispense with full powers.

Thus the general rule is expressed in suitably flexible terms. Subparagraph (*b*) is intended to preserve the modern practice of States to dispense with full powers in the case of agreements in simplified form. At the first session of the conference a proposal to delete this particular provision was defeated. It was argued in favour of deletion that the provision 'by creating a presumption of authority to conclude a treaty could have the effect of binding a State without its Government being even aware that a binding commitment was being undertaken on the State's behalf'.[3] In reply it was pointed out that the essential idea was that normally full powers were required, but that the States engaged in the negotiations could

[3] *Official Records, First Session*, 13th meeting (Carmona).

agree to dispense with them if it became apparent that the results of the negotiations could be incorporated in an agreement in simplified form; in such circumstances 'the onus was on the negotiators to see that they were qualified to bind their respective States'.[4]

In their commentary to the draft article which eventually emerged (with some minor modification) as Article 7 of the Convention, the Commission pointed out that the general rule 'makes it clear that the production of full powers is the fundamental safeguard for the representatives of the States concerned of each other's qualifications to represent their State for the purpose of performing the particular act in question'.[5] Implicitly, therefore, the Commission recognized that the non-production of full powers might involve a certain risk for one or other of the States concerned, in the sense that it might be subsequently claimed that an act relating to the conclusion of a treaty had been performed without authority.

Partly to guard against this risk and also to respect accepted international practice, paragraph 2 of Article 7 of the Convention establishes that, 'in virtue of their functions and without having to produce full powers', Heads of State, Heads of Government and Ministers for Foreign Affairs are considered as representing their State for the purpose of all acts relating to the conclusion of a treaty. Heads of diplomatic missions are likewise considered as representing their State *ex officio* and without the need to produce full powers, but only for the purpose of adopting the text of a treaty between the accrediting State and the State to which they are accredited. Finally, representatives accredited by States to an international conference or to an international organisation or one of its organs enjoy similar powers, but only for the purpose of adopting the text of a treaty in that conference, organisation or organ.

An interesting point which was raised at the conference is the relationship between this rule about inherent capacity to perform certain acts relating to the conclusion of treaties and the rule set out in Article 46 of the Convention concerning the violation of provisions of internal law regarding competence to conclude treaties. It will be recalled that Article 46 establishes the principle that a State may not invoke the fact that its consent to be bound by a treaty has been expressed in violation of a provision of its internal law regarding competence to conclude treaties unless that violation was manifest and concerned a rule of its internal law of fundamental

[4] *Loc. cit.* (Jagota).

[5] 1966 I.L.C. Reports, p. 26.

importance. The question is: does paragraph 2 of Article 7 raise an incontestable presumption as a matter of international law that the designated office-holders are *ex officio* entitled to perform the specified acts without the need to produce full powers notwithstanding that, as a matter of internal law, they are not empowered to do so? It would seem that the presumption is incontestable. A proposal at the first session of the conference to include a reference to internal law in the text of Article 7 was not pressed to a vote. Furthermore, the point at issue had already been covered by the Commission in their commentary to what is now Article 46. In discussing the doctrine that internal laws limiting the powers of State organs to enter into treaties may render voidable any consent given on the international plane in disregard of a constitutional limitation, the Commission had specifically stated, in rejecting that doctrine:

> If this view were to be accepted, it would follow that other States would not be entitled to rely on the authority to commit the State ostensibly possessed by a Head of State, Prime Minister, Foreign Minister, etc., under Article [7]; they would have to satisfy themselves in each case that the provisions of the State's constitution are not infringed or take the risk of subsequently finding the treaty void.[6]

Article 8 of the Convention forms the corollary to Article 7. It provides that an act relating to the conclusion of a treaty performed by a person who cannot be considered under Article 7 as authorised to represent a State for that purpose is without legal effect unless afterwards confirmed by that State. Cases of this kind are, of course, very rare, but the Commission's commentary cites two or three relevant examples from diplomatic history where State representatives had signed treaties in the absence of authority to do so. The *rationale* of the rule embodied in Article 8 would appear to be, as the Commission suggest, that 'where there is no authority to enter into a treaty . . . the State must be entitled to disavow the act of its representative'.[7] An important point, which the text of Article 8 does not entirely resolve, is whether the subsequent confirmation must be expressed or can be implied from the conduct of the State concerned. The drafting history demonstrates fairly conclusively that confirmation can be so implied. In the first place, the Commis-

[6] *Loc. cit.*, pp. 69–70. For a contrary view, see Hostert, 'Droit international et droit interne', *Annuaire Français de Droit International* (1969), p. 108.

[7] *Loc. cit.*, p. 27.

sion, in their commentary to the provision on which Article 8 is based, state explicitly that a State will be held to have endorsed the unauthorised act of its representative by implication if it invokes the provisions of the treaty or otherwise acts in such a way as to appear to treat the act of its representative as effective.[8] In the second place, an amendment proposed by Venezuela at the first session of the conference requiring confirmation to be express was decisively rejected on the grounds *inter alia* that 'confirmation implied by the silence of the State in question was recognised in practice'[9] and that 'there was no objection to providing for tacit confirmation from the behaviour of the State concerned'.[10]

2 ADOPTION AND AUTHENTICATION OF THE TEXT OF A TREATY

The next stage in the conclusion of a treaty is the adoption of the text. In the Convention itself there is no definition of the term 'adoption', but it would appear to mean the formal act whereby the form and content of the proposed treaty are settled.[11] Historically, the adoption of the text of a treaty took place by the agreement of all the States participating in the negotiations. Unanimity could therefore be said to constitute the classical rule—a rule which was considered so obvious as hardly to require stating in terms.

Unanimity must, by the nature of things, remain the unqualified rule for the adoption of the text of a bilateral treaty. If the parties to a proposed bilateral treaty have not reached agreement on the terms of the treaty, there is self-evidently no *consensus ad idem* and no text to be 'adopted'. The negotiations will obviously continue until the outstanding points in dispute have been settled and the necessary wording for the treaty agreed upon.

Unanimity likewise remains the rule for the category of treaties known, for purposes of convenience, as 'restricted multilateral treaties'. A 'restricted multilateral treaty' may be defined as a treaty

[8] *Ibid.* [9] *Official Records, First Session,* 14th meeting (Blix).

[10] *Loc. cit.* (Ruda). It should be noted that a Malaysian proposal to insert the words 'expressly or by necessary implication' in the text of Article 8 was likewise defeated. As objection had been made to the word 'necessary', it may be inferred not only that confirmation may be implied, but also that the implication need not be a 'necessary' one.

[11] 1966 I.L.C. Reports, p. 27.

whose object and purpose are such that the application of the treaty in its entirety between all the parties is an essential condition of the consent of each one to be bound by the treaty.[12] Examples of restricted multilateral treaties are treaties establishing very close co-operation between a limited number of States, such as treaties of economic integration, treaties between riparian States relating to the development of a river basin or treaties relating to the building of a hydro-electric dam, scientific installations or the like.[13] Treaties of this nature, particularly treaties providing for economic integration, are of growing significance in current practice. The most notable illustration is the series of treaties providing for the establishment of the European Communities. The essential characteristic of such treaties is that they incorporate a nexus of clearly interdependent rights and obligations, the fulfilment of which in their entirety by all the States involved is a precondition for the staged progress towards the objectives set out in the treaty. Thus unanimity remains the rule for the adoption of the text of such a treaty, and unanimity remains the rule for its entry into force.[14] In principle, unanimity is also required for the admission of a new member to a grouping of this nature, in the sense that the consent of all the original member States, as well as of the applicant State, to be bound by an agreement embodying conditions of admission is required as a condition precedent to admission.[15]

[12] There is no definition of the term as such in the Vienna Convention. France proposed a definition of the expression at the first session of the Vienna conference (A/Conf. 39/C.1/L.24), but withdrew this proposal at the opening of the second session; see M. Hubert's statement at the 84th meeting of the Committee of the Whole, recorded in *Official Records, Second Session*, p. 213. The definition suggested is based on the wording of Article 20(2) of the Vienna Convention, which makes it clear that reservations to restricted multilateral treaties require acceptance by all the parties.

[13] *Official Records, First Session*, 4th meeting (Virally).

[14] In this connection, note the terms of Article 247 of the E.E.C. Treaty and Article 224 of the Euratom Treaty.

[15] Article 237, E.E.C. Treaty, and Article 205, Euratom Treaty. But where there is more than one applicant State, and the conditions of admission are settled within the framework of a multilateral agreement adopted by the original member States and the applicant States, the agreement may exceptionally authorise entry into force on condition that all the original member States and at least one applicant State ratify it. In such circumstances, there will obviously be a need, because of the close interdependence of the treaty provisions and the fact that they have been drawn up on the assumption that all applicant

Article 9 of the Convention accordingly sets out, in paragraph 1, the general rule that the adoption of the text of a treaty takes place by the consent of the States participating in its drawing up. But it is obvious that this rule is not appropriate to the process whereby the texts of treaties are adopted at international conferences. Accordingly, Article 9 (2) of the Convention establishes the general rule that 'the adoption of the text of a treaty at an international conference takes place by the vote of two-thirds of the States present and voting unless by the same majority they shall decide to apply a different rule'.

We have already noted that this particular provision constitutes progressive development rather than codification.[16] At the conference some doubts were expressed about the substance of this rule, particularly in view of the differing types of international conference to which it might be thought to be applicable. At the first session the delegation of Austria drew attention to the fact 'no criterion qualifying an international conference emerges from the commentary to paragraph 2'.[17] The representative of Iraq (himself a member of the International Law Commission) commented that the rule laid down in paragraph 2 'was in fact followed only at major conferences and it would therefore be desirable to insert the word "general" before "international conference"'.[18] There was general agreement that the rule set out in Article 9(2) did not automatically apply to treaties adopted within international organisations if the relevant rules of the organisation provided otherwise; in their comments on what is now Article 5 of the Convention, representatives of such disparate international organisations as the F.A.O., the Council of Europe, the League of Arab States, B.I.R.P.I. (International Bureaux for the Protection of Intellectual and Industrial Property) and the International Bank had all pointed to the existence of rules or practices operating within their organisations which

---

States will join the grouping, to make certain indispensable adaptations to the treaty. For an interesting example of this exceptional type of arrangement, see Article 2 of the Treaty concerning the Accession of the Kingdom of Denmark, Ireland, the Kingdom of Norway and the United Kingdom of Great Britain and Northern Ireland to the European Economic Community, signed at Brussels on 22 January 1972 (Cmnd. 4862—I).

[16] *Supra*, p. 14.

[17] *Official Records, First Session,* 15th meeting (Zemanek).

[18] *Loc. cit.* (Yasseen).

were, or might be, contrary to the general rule proposed for the adoption of the text of a treaty at an international conference.

It would accordingly seem that the rule set out in Article 9(2) applies essentially to major international conferences—that is to say, large conferences attended by a great number of States. If such conferences are convened within the framework of international organisations, then any special rules of the organisation for the adoption of treaties will apply, notwithstanding Article 9(2); and the only remaining point of doubt would appear to be whether the rule in Article 9(2) applies to regional conferences organised independently of regional organisations. The answer would appear to be that suggested by Sir Humphrey Waldock and endorsed by the Commission, when considering, at an earlier stage, certain governmental comments—namely, that Article 9(2) does in principle apply to regional conferences, but that such a conference can always decide, by a two-thirds majority, to apply the unanimity rule.[19]

Article 10 of the Convention, relating to authentication, requires little comment. It should be noted that this rule relates to the establishment as authentic and definitive of the *text* of a treaty. It is a common feature of international negotiations, as the United States government pointed out in written comments to an early draft prepared by the Commission, that 'in some instances, initialling [a text] merely constitutes agreement by the representatives negotiating the treaty that they have reached agreement upon a particular text to refer to their respective governments for consideration'.[20] Following upon this and other comments, the Commission undertook a redraft of the rule. There seems little risk that the text of Article 10, as finally adopted, could be interpreted as applying to the initialling of drafts by negotiators at some midway stage in the negotiations for the purpose of consultation with governments. Where negotiations are interrupted for this purpose, it will normally be quite clear what

[19] The Luxembourg government had pointed out the unsuitability of applying the two-thirds voting rule to regional conferences; see comment to Article 6 of the 1962 I.L.C. draft, reproduced in 1966 I.L.C. Reports. Sir Humphrey Waldock, in his 'Fourth Report on the Law of Treaties' (A/CN.4/177 of 19 March 1965), maintained that 'if, in a "regional" conference, unanimity is the only acceptable voting rule the States participating will have no difficulty in arriving at a decision, by the two-thirds majority procedural vote . . . to apply the unanimity rule' (p. 58).

[20] 1966 I.L.C. Reports, pp. 171–2.

is the precise status of the texts and the act of initialling at this particular stage ought not to be capable of being confused with authentication as such.

3 EXPRESSION OF CONSENT TO BE BOUND BY A TREATY

Articles 11–17 of the Convention are concerned with the means by which States express their consent to be bound by a treaty. Article 11, which is a new article adopted at the conference on a proposal by Poland and the United States, lists the various means as 'signature, exchange of instruments constituting a treaty, ratification, acceptance, approval or accession, or . . . any other means if so agreed'. The Commission had not thought it necessary to put forward such a general rule on the means of expressing consent to be bound, nor had it suggested any specific provision for the expression of consent to be bound by a treaty to be effected by means of an exchange of instruments. The conference decided otherwise, no doubt influenced by the growing practice of constituting treaties by an exchange of unsigned *notes verbales*.

The major issue which arises on this series of articles is, however, the question whether, in the absence of an express provision to that effect, treaties require ratification. There has been a long-standing doctrinal argument on this point. On the one hand, McNair[21] and the Harvard Research[22] had taken the view that ratification is required when the treaty or the attendant circumstances do not indicate an intention to dispense with ratification. As against this, Fitzmaurice, writing in 1934, had expressed the view that 'the necessity for ratification is not inherent and depends in the last resort, not on any general rules, but on the intention of the parties; and that where no intention to ratify is apparent it may be assumed that none exists'.[23] Blix, in more recent years, after an extensive review of modern State practice, had concluded that 'whenever States intend to bring treaties into force by some procedure other than signature, that intention is evidenced by express provisions or by cogent implication' and that 'in the present practice of States

[21] *Op. cit.*, p. 133.

[22] 29 *A.J.I.L.* Supplement (1935), p. 763. In support of this view, the Harvard Research cites Crandall, *Treaties: their Making and Enforcement* (1916), p. 2, Hall, *International Law,* eighth edition (1924), s. 110, and various other writers.

[23] Fitzmaurice, 'Do treaties need ratification?' in 15 *B.Y.I.L.* (1934), p. 129.

the treaties in which there is no clear evidence, express or implied, of the parties' intentions as to the mode of entry into force, almost without exception enter into force by signature'.[24]

The Commission had clearly been rather perplexed as to how to handle this potentially divisive issue. In 1962 the Commission had adopted a rather complex preliminary draft article to the effect that 'treaties in principle require ratification unless they fall within one of the exceptions . . . below'. But this had encountered opposition from a number of States, such as Denmark, Japan, Sweden and the United Kingdom, who had suggested that the presumption should be reversed. Other States had criticised the wording of the exceptions, and yet others suggested that the Commission need not adopt a position on the doctrinal issue. In the light of these developments the Commission reconstructed the draft article so as 'simply to set out the conditions under which the consent of a State to be bound by a treaty is expressed by ratification in modern international law' and 'to leave the question of ratification as a matter of the intention of the negotiating States without recourse to a statement of a controversial residuary rule'.[25]

Thus the Commission had avoided the crucial issue of whether, when a treaty is silent on the matter, the consent of a State to be bound is expressed by signature or by ratification. But it had done so deliberately, drawing attention to the fact that treaties normally either provide that the instrument shall be ratified or, by laying down that the treaty shall enter into force upon signature or upon a specific date or event, dispense with ratification, and that accordingly 'total silence on the subject is exceptional'. This is confirmed by the analysis made by Blix, who points out that, of the 1,300 instruments reproduced in the United Nations Treaty Series between 1946 and 1951, at least 1,125 expressly or by clear implication state the manner by which they are to come into force.[26]

At the conference, however, the issue was not so easily disposed of. At the first session there was a lengthy discussion on whether there should be incorporated in the Convention a residuary rule in favour of signature or of ratification when a treaty was silent as to how consent to be bound should be expressed. Czechoslovakia, Poland and Sweden tabled an amendment favouring signature as

[24] Blix, 'The requirement of ratification' in 30 *B.Y.I.L.* (1953), p. 380.
[25] 1966 I.L.C. Reports, p. 31.
[26] *Loc. cit.*, pp. 359–60.

the residuary rule; and a group of nine Latin American States tabled an amendment establishing ratification as the residuary rule. The discussion revealed very little in the way of new argument. The proponents of ratification as the residuary rule stressed that this would have the advantage of order and certainty and would ensure compliance with internal constitutional requirements. The proponents of signature as the residuary rule insisted that this reflected the current practice of States, given the tendency towards the conclusion of agreements in simplified form (e.g. exchanges of notes) not requiring ratification. In the event the debate was inconclusive; of some thirty speakers, ten expressed themselves (sometimes with qualifications) in favour of a residuary rule of signature,[27] thirteen favoured a residuary rule of ratification[28] and seven adopted an indeterminate position.[29] The sponsors of the amendment favouring a residuary rule of signature thereupon withdrew their proposal, and the Latin American amendment calling for a residuary rule of ratification was defeated by a vote of twenty-five in favour and fifty-three against, with sixteen abstentions.[30] Thus the Convention, as adopted, makes no attempt to resolve the doctrinal dispute of whether there should be a presumption in favour of signature or ratification as a means of expressing a State's consent to be bound when the treaty is silent on the matter. It simply enumerates the circumstances in which consent to be bound is expressed by signature and the circumstances in which consent to be bound is expressed by ratification.

4 OBLIGATION NOT TO DEFEAT THE OBJECT AND PURPOSE OF A TREATY

As has already been indicated, the treaty-making process involves a number of stages. The penultimate stage is the period between signature of a treaty (assuming the treaty is subject to ratification)

[27] The representatives of Czechoslovakia, Poland, South Africa, the United Kingdom, Denmark, Hungary, the Federal Republic of Germany, Sweden, Japan and Australia.

[28] The representatives of Venezuela, Switzerland, Uruguay, Bulgaria, Iraq, Guinea, Iran, France, Ethiopia, Turkey, Greece, the Congo (Brazzaville) and India.

[29] The representatives of Romania, Israel, Ghana, Italy, Yugoslavia, Nigeria and Brazil.

[30] *Official Records, First Session,* 18th meeting, pp. 94–5.

and entry into force, or between ratification and entry into force (in circumstances where entry into force is conditional upon the deposit of a specified number of instruments of ratification). Article 18 of the Convention lays down the rule that 'a State is obliged to refrain from acts which would defeat the object and purpose of a treaty' during this grey period preceding entry into force.

The point has already been made that this provision in all probability constitutes at least a measure of progressive development, although there is some inchoate authority for the proposition that States which have signed a treaty subject to ratification must observe certain restraints on their activities during the period preceding entry into force, particularly if those activities would render the performance by any party of the obligations stipulated in the treaty impossible or more difficult.[31] As Anzilotti puts it:

> Il faut encore observer que, en excluant tout effet obligatoire du traité antérieurement à la ratification, on ne veut pas dire que l'Etat puisse ne tenir aucun compte du texte intervenu et faire comme si rien ne s'était produit. Il y a lieu, par contre, d'admettre que, lorsque la procédure de ratification d'un traité régulièrement signé est pendante, l'Etat doit s'abstenir d'accomplir des actes de nature à rendre impossible ou plus difficile l'exécution régulière du traité une fois ratifié. Mais il est clair qu'il ne s'agit pas alors d'un effet du traité comme tel mais bien d'une application du principe qui défend d'abuser du droit.[32]

McNair also cites a certain amount of material, much of which he concedes to be somewhat inconclusive, in support of the proposition that 'States which have signed a treaty requiring ratification have thereby placed certain limitations upon their freedom of action during the period which precedes its entry into force'.[33]

It should be noted that the final draft article submitted by the Commission in 1966 stated the nature of the obligation as an obligation 'to refrain from acts *tending to frustrate* the object of a proposed treaty'. At the conference this phraseology was modified to refer to an obligation 'to refrain from acts *which would defeat the object and purpose* of a treaty'. The phrase 'tending to frustrate' had been criticised by a number of delegations, including those of the United Kingdom, the United States, Ghana and Uruguay and, although the

[31] Cf Article 9 of the Harvard Research draft, *loc. cit.*, pp. 778–87.
[32] *Cours de Droit International*, Gidel translation (1929), pp. 372–3.
[33] *Op. cit.*, p. 199.

Expert Consultant, Sir Humphrey Waldock, explained that the phrase 'was based on a well established notion in English law' and meant simply that 'the treaty was rendered meaningless by such acts and lost its object',[34] it was clearly felt desirable to tighten up the language employed. The modification was accordingly proposed by the Drafting Committee, and accepted without any material comment.

Specific treaty provisions do, of course, occasionally seek to give some kind of material content to the general principle expressed in Article 18 of the Convention. There is, for example, an implicit acknowledgment of the principle involved in the instrument entitled 'Procedure for the Adoption of Certain Decisions and Other Measures to be taken during the Period preceding Accession' which is annexed to the Final Act signed simultaneously with the Treaty concerning the Accession of Denmark, Ireland, Norway and the United Kingdom to the European Economic Community and the European Atomic Energy Community. This instrument, which for purposes of convenience I will style the 'interim procedure document', provides that, during the period preceding accession, any proposal or communication from the Commission of the European Communities which might lead to decisions by the Council of these Communities shall be brought to the attention of the acceding States. Elaborate arrangements are then made for consultations at various levels. Conversely, it is provided that the procedures for consultation shall also apply to any decision to be taken by the acceding States which might affect the commitments resulting from their position as future members of the Communities.[35] In this way, practical consultation procedures are envisaged in order to ensure that on neither side will action be taken which would defeat, or render substantially more difficult of accomplishment, the object and purpose of the Treaty of Accession, namely, the enlargement of the European Communities.

II RESERVATIONS

The Convention regime on reservations is set out in Articles 19–23. I do not propose to sketch out the historical background. This has effectively been done in the commentary to the final set of draft

[34] *Official Records, First Session,* 20th meeting.

[35] Miscellaneous No. 3 (1972)—Part I: Cmnd. 4862—I, p. 128.

articles submitted by the International Law Commission in 1966.[36] It is sufficient to note that the classical 'unanimity rule' according to which a reservation proposed to a multilateral Convention requires the acceptance, express or tacit, of all States having a legitimate interest in the Convention had been substantially eroded following the advisory opinion given by the International Court in 1951 in the 'Genocide Convention' case.[37] As against this, there had been little or no increased support for the opposed extreme position that every State has an absolute right to make reservations at will and to become a party to a multilateral Convention subject to such reservations and notwithstanding any objections made. Instead, the practice of the Secretary-General (the principal depository of multilateral Conventions) had evolved in the direction of simply acting as a channel for the receipt and transmission of instruments containing reservations or objections to reservations, without drawing any legal consequences from such instruments. This practice of the Secretary-General was based on General Assembly resolution 598 (VI), which had requested the Secretary-General, with regard to future multilateral Conventions concluded under the auspices of the United Nations of which he is the depository:

(*a*) to continue to act as depository in connection with the deposit of documents containing reservations or objections, without passing upon the legal effect of such documents; and
(*b*) to communicate the text of such documents relating to reservations or objections to all States concerned, leaving it to each State to draw legal consequences from such communications.

The proposals submitted by the Commission, which were in large measure accepted by the conference and incorporated in the Convention, were, with certain qualifications, based on the pan-American doctrine. Thus the Convention regime may be summarised as follows:

(*a*) States are entitled to formulate a reservation on signature or ratification of a treaty unless the treaty prohibits reservations or provides that only specified reservations, which do not include the reservation in question, may be made.

[36] 1966 I.L.C. Reports, pp. 35–40. See also Sinclair, 'The Vienna Conference on the Law of Treaties', 19 *I.C.L.Q.* (1970), pp. 53–60, and Kearney and Dalton, *loc. cit.*, pp. 509–14.
[37] *I.C.J. Reports* (1951), p. 15.

(*b*) Where the treaty is silent on reservations, States are entitled to formulate a reservation unless the reservation is incompatible with the object and purpose of the treaty. (This is the test laid down in the 'Genocide Convention' case.)

(*c*) Reservations to a restricted multilateral treaty require acceptance by all the parties, and reservations to a constituent instrument of an international organisation require the acceptance of the competent organ of that organisation, unless the treaty otherwise provides.

(*d*) In other cases, and unless the particular treaty otherwise provides:

(i) The express or tacit acceptance of a reservation by another contracting State constitutes the reserving State a party to the treaty in relation to that other State, tacit acceptance being assumed if no objection is raised within a specified period.

(ii) An objection to a reservation by another contracting State does not preclude the entry into force of the treaty as between the objecting and reserving States unless a contrary intention is definitely expressed by the objecting State.

(iii) An act expressing a State's consent to be bound by a treaty which contains a reservation is effective as soon as at least one other contracting State has accepted the reservation.

This is the broad effect of Articles 19 and 20 of the Convention. There are some minor variations from the proposals submitted by the Commission in 1966, the most significant being the reversal of the rule concerning the legal effect of an objection to a reservation. The Commission had put forward the rule that an objection to a reservation precludes the entry into force of a treaty as between the objecting and reserving States unless a contrary intention is expressed by the objecting State. The conference, on the basis of a proposal by the Soviet Union at the second session, put the onus on the objecting State to declare positively that its objection had the effect of precluding entry into force. At the conclusion of the short debate on the Soviet amendment at the second session, the Expert Consultant, Sir Humphrey Waldock, stated:

. . . the problem was merely that of formulating a rule one way or the other. The essential aim was to have a stated rule as a guide to the conduct of States, and from the point of view of substance it was doubtful if there was any very great consideration in favour of stating the rule in one way rather than the other, provided it was perfectly clear.[38]

Notwithstanding the force of this argument, the reversal of the rule will unquestionably have some consequences for the future. The most significant feature of international practice concerning reservations is the part played by tacit consent. Tacit consent is, of course, presumed from failure to object to a reservation, and provision is made for this in the Convention. But the reversal of the rule concerning the legal effect of an objection to a reservation enlarges the role played by tacit consent; for even an objection to a reservation will not bring about the absence of treaty relations between the objecting and reserving States, unless the objecting State specifically declares that this is the effect of the objection. Furthermore, objections to reservations have frequently been made in the past in an endeavour to persuade the reserving State to withdraw its reservation; the pressure to withdraw will now be slight if the treaty may enter into force between the objecting and reserving States in any case. Finally, there is the psychological consideration that the onus is now on the innocent party (that is to say, the objecting State) to declare publicly that it does not intend to have treaty relations with the reserving State; this is an onus which smaller States may find difficult to discharge when the reserving State is a powerful neighbour.

It may be argued that these considerations are theoretical. But we already have some experience as to how the Convention regime on reservations will operate. The Vienna conference decided, in full knowledge of the consequences, that it would not have a separate provision governing reservations to the Convention itself.[39] Articles 19–23 of the Convention accordingly apply to reservations to the Convention itself.

[38] *Official Records, Second Session,* 10th plenary meeting.

[39] A specific proposal by Spain to prohibit reservations to Part V of the Convention was rejected by sixty-two votes to nine, with thirty-three abstentions in the concluding stages of the conference, after strong objections had been voiced by the delegations of Brazil, Israel, the Soviet Union, India, the United Kingdom and Nigeria; see *Official Records, Second Session,* 34th plenary meeting, paras. 93–102.

A number of declarations and reservations have been made by various States on signature of the Convention, and still more have been made on ratification or accession.[40] It will be noted that, on signature, declarations or reservations were appended by Afghanistan, Bolivia, Costa Rica, Ecuador, the Federal Republic of Germany, Guatemala, Morocco and the United Kingdom. In depositing their instruments of ratification or accession, Canada, New Zealand and the United Kingdom have appended declarations, and Syria and Tunisia have appended reservations.

In analysing the legal effect of these declarations and reservations in the light of the provisions of the Vienna Convention, it is first of all necessary to be quite clear as to what is a reservation. A reservation is defined in Article 2(1)(d) of the Convention as 'a unilateral statement, however phrased or named, made by a State, when signing, ratifying, accepting, approving or acceding to a treaty, *whereby it purports to exclude or to modify the legal effect of certain provisions of the treaty in their application to that State*'. I have stressed the legal characteristics of a reservation, since it will be apparent that many of the declarations appended on signature, and some of the declarations appended on ratification or accession, do not constitute reservations *stricto sensu*. They are rather in the nature of political statements, setting out the views of the government concerned on broad or particular issues, or they are in the nature of interpretative declarations, stating the understanding of the government concerned as to how certain provisions of the Convention will be applied.

As a prime example of a declaration appended on signature which in reality is in the nature of a political statement, I would cite the declaration made by Bolivia to the effect that 'the shortcomings of the Vienna Convention are such as to postpone the realisation of the aspirations of mankind' but that 'nevertheless, the rules endorsed by the Convention do represent significant advances, based on the principles of international justice which Bolivia has traditionally supported'.

Examples of declarations appended on signature or ratification which are in the nature of interpretative declarations are more

[40] Full details of these declarations and reservations will be found in Miscellaneous No. 19 (1971): Cmnd. 4818, which is a republication of the Vienna Convention, with details of all signatures and of ratifications, accessions, reservations and declarations received up to November 1971.

numerous. There is first the declaration made by Afghanistan stating its understanding that sub-paragraph 2(a) of Article 62, concerning fundamental changes of circumstances, 'does not cover unequal and illegal treaties or any treaties contrary to the principle of self-determination'.[41] There is, second, the declaration made by Ecuador on signature, incorporating the understanding of the government of that country about the effect of Article 4 of the Vienna Convention. And there is, third, the declaration made by the United Kingdom on signature and confirmed on ratification about the relationship between Article 66 of the Convention and the United Kingdom's acceptance of the compulsory jurisdiction of the International Court of Justice.[42]

It may be permissible to say something in explanation of the United Kingdom declaration. Article 66 of the Vienna Convention (which I will discuss in more detail later) provides for reference to the International Court, at the instance of any of the parties, of any dispute concerning the interpretation or application of the articles relating to *jus cogens*; and for compulsory conciliation in relation to disputes concerning the interpretation or application of any of the other articles in Part V of the Convention. But the report of the conciliation commission provided for under the Annex to the Convention is not to be binding upon the parties; it is to have 'no other character than that of recommendations submitted for the consideration of the parties in order to facilitate an amicable settlement of the dispute'.[43] Now sub-paragraph (i)(a) of the declaration made by the United Kingdom government on 1 January 1969 accepting as compulsory the jurisdiction of the International Court of Justice had specifically excluded 'any dispute which the United Kingdom . . . has agreed with the other Party or Parties thereto to settle by some other method of peaceful settlement'.[44] Conciliation may, in principle, be regarded as another method of peaceful settlement, but the difficulty is that the procedures for conciliation laid down in the Annex to the Convention may not lead to a settlement, since the report of the conciliation commission is not binding

[41] A similar declaration was made on signature by Morocco; see Cmnd. 4818, p. 47.

[42] Similar declarations were made on ratification and accession by the governments of New Zealand and Canada respectively.

[43] Paragraph 6 of the Annex to the Vienna Convention.

[44] I.C.J. *Yearbook* (1970–71), p. 72.

on the parties, and no provision is made for further action in the event of the conciliation effort being unsuccessful. Against this background, the United Kingdom government was clearly anxious to ensure that, *vis-à-vis* States parties to the Vienna Convention who had accepted as compulsory the jurisdiction of the International Court, the combined effect of Article 66 of the Convention and of the terms of the United Kingdom optional clause declaration should not be such as to oust the jurisdiction of the Court.

I turn now to what are clearly intended to be reservations in the strict sense. For the time being we can ignore those made on signature, and not yet confirmed on ratification, since Article 23(2) of the Convention provides that a reservation formulated on signature must be formally confirmed by the reserving State when expressing its consent to be bound by the treaty and that, in such a case, the reservation shall be considered as having been made on the date of its confirmation. Reservations in the strict sense have been made on signature by Costa Rica and Guatemala, seeking to preserve certain constitutional provisions as against the terms of the Convention or otherwise to vary or modify those terms; but, as neither Costa Rica nor Guatemala has yet sought to ratify the Convention, no occasion has yet arisen for other States to take a final position on these reservations.

Finally, and most significantly, one must consider what has been the reaction to the reservations formulated by States on ratification or accession. Here one must draw attention to the reservations formulated by Syria when acceding to the Convention on 2 October 1970. They are five in number and require careful analysis. First, there is a declaration that acceptance of the Convention by Syria does not signify recognition of Israel. Second, there is a political statement (which clearly does not amount to a reservation in the strict sense) that Article 81 is not in conformity with the aims and purposes of the Convention in that it does not allow all States, without distinction or discrimination, to become parties to it. Third, there is an interpretative declaration stating that the Syrian government interpret the expression 'threat or use of force' as used in Article 52 of the Convention as extending also to the employment of economic, political, military or psychological coercion and to all types of coercion constraining a State to conclude a treaty against its wishes or its interests. Fourth, there is a specific reservation (in the strict sense) stating that the Syrian government does not accept the non-applicability of the principle of a fundamental change of circumstances with regard to treaties establishing boundaries, despite the terms of Article 62(2)(a) of the Convention. Finally, and most significantly, there is a general reservation stating that the accession of Syria to the Convention shall not apply to the Annex to the Convention, which concerns obligatory conciliation.

What has been the reaction of other States to this series of interpretative declarations and reservations? It should be noted initially that the principle of tacit consent as formulated in the Convention is to the effect that a reservation is considered to have been accepted by a State if it raises no objection by the end of a period of twelve months after notification of the reservation or by the date on which it expresses its consent to be bound by the treaty, *whichever is later*. Accordingly, the vast majority of States who participated in the conference have not yet been obliged to take a position on the Syrian reservations and will not be so obliged until they ratify or accede to the Convention.

Two States have taken a position on the Syrian reservations—the United Kingdom and the United States. The United Kingdom was obliged to consider carefully the terms of the Syrian reservations at the time of the deposit of its instrument of ratification, since failure to register an objection within a year of notification of the Syrian accession would have meant that the United Kingdom accepted the Syrian reservations.

In the event, the United Kingdom declaration appended to its instrument of ratification contains two observations on the Syrian reservations. First, and with reference to the Syrian interpretative declaration on Article 52, the declaration records that 'the United Kingdom does not accept that the interpretation of Article 52 put forward by the Government of Syria correctly reflects the conclusions reached at the Conference of Vienna on the subject of coercion; the Conference dealt with this matter by adopting a Declaration on this subject which forms part of the Final Act'. Second, and of immeasurably greater significance, the United Kingdom formally lodged an objection to the reservation entered by the government of Syria in respect of the Annex to the Convention and declared that it did not accept the entry into force of the Convention as between the United Kingdom and Syria.[45]

Why was this serious step taken? As I shall be demonstrating at

[45] Cmnd. 4818, p. 53.

a later stage, the dominant issue at the conference was the relationship between the series of articles relating to the invalidity, termination and suspension of operation of treaties and the provisions to be written into the Convention concerning the settlement of disputes arising on the interpretation or application of these articles. A majority of States represented at the conference (including the United Kingdom) were not prepared to commit themselves to the degree of progressive development represented by Part V of the Convention, and in particular by the sometimes vague and ill-defined grounds of invalidity, without an assurance that there would be automatically available procedures for the settlement of disputes when a ground of invalidity was invoked. Article 66 of the Convention represented the hard-won and vital compromise on this dominant issue. It can be assumed that the United Kingdom took the view that a reservation to Article 66 the effect of which would be to exclude the procedures for compulsory conciliation set out in the Annex was incompatible with the object and purpose of the Convention, since, to use the words of the International Law Commission, it 'undermined the basis of the treaty or of a compromise made in the negotiations'.[46] The Syrian reservation on this point accordingly struck at the roots of the compromise solution agreed upon with such difficulty at the Vienna conference, and it is not surprising that the United Kingdom exercised its right under Article 20 of the Convention to declare that the effect of its objection was to preclude the entry into force of the Vienna Convention as between the United Kingdom and Syria.

In view of the objection taken by the United Kingdom to the Syrian reservation to the Annex to the Convention, and the legal effect of that objection, it was unnecessary for the United Kingdom to express a view on the specific Syrian reservation to Article 62(2)(a).

The United States government were under no such compulsion as the United Kingdom to declare their position with respect to the Syrian reservations, since the United States have not yet ratified the Convention. Yet they have taken such a position, which, interestingly, differs from that of the United Kingdom. The United States government, in a note addressed to the Secretary-General on 26 May 1971, have stated their view that the Syrian reservation to the Annex to the Convention 'is incompatible with the object

[46] 1966 I.L.C. Reports, p. 37.

and purpose of impartial settlement of disputes'. The note continues as follows:

The United States Government intends, at such time as it may become a party to the Vienna Convention on the Law of Treaties, to reaffirm its objection to the foregoing reservation and to reject treaty relations with the Syrian Arab Republic under all provisions in Part V of the Convention with regard to which the Syrian Arab Republic has rejected the obligatory conciliation procedures set forth in the Annex to the Convention.[47]

The effect of this objection would appear to be that, as between the United States and Syria, Parts I–IV and Parts VI–VIII of the Vienna Convention will apply if or when the United States becomes a party to the Convention, but Part V will not apply, with the possible exception of Articles 53, 64 and 66(a).

The United States objection raises one interesting doctrinal point. As will be recalled, Article 20(4)(b) gives the objecting State an option to declare that the effect of its objection is to preclude the entry into force of the treaty as between the objecting and reserving States. Can this be utilised by the objecting State to preclude treaty relations only as regards part of a treaty? This is untested ground, but in principle there would appear to be no reason why an objection to a reservation may not produce this effect, provided the treaty is of such a nature that separability of its provisions is a practicable proposition. One could possibly apply here by analogy the terms of Article 44(3) of the Convention. The analogy is all the more apt since, as I have already indicated, the inclusion of automatically available procedures for the settlement of Part V disputes was an essential basis of the consent of many States to be bound by the series of substantive articles on the invalidity, termination and suspension of operation of treaties. It would seem to follow from the nature of the United States objection that Syria would be entitled to refuse treaty relations with the United States on the basis set out in the United States note, since the objection in essence amounts to an offer of treaty relations on a limited scale.

The application of the Convention regime on reservations so far does not permit of any definite conclusions. It remains to be seen whether the greater liberality which the regime affords to the formulation of reservations will be abused. There is a real danger

[47] Cmnd. 4818, p. 54.

that too lax an attitude towards the formulation and acceptance of reservations will result in the fractionalisation of treaty regimes agreed upon only with great difficulty. The assumed advantage of a more flexible reservations regime is that it will encourage a larger number of States to become parties to multilateral Conventions; but this advantage will be more than counterbalanced if the effect of greater liberality is to destroy, or to undermine, the fundamental basis of the treaty itself.

III ENTRY INTO FORCE AND PROVISIONAL APPLICATION OF TREATIES

I can be brief on Articles 24 and 25 of the Convention, which deal with the entry into force and provisional application of treaties.

Article 24 lays down the unexceptionable rule that a treaty enters into force in such manner and upon such date as it may provide or as the negotiating States may agree; and that, failing any such provision or agreement, a treaty enters into force as soon as consent to be bound by the treaty has been established for all the negotiating States. Consent to be bound can, of course, be expressed by any of the means specified in Article 11 of the Convention, depending on the terms of the treaty concerned.

What is now paragraph 4 of Article 24 of the Convention is an addition to the Commission proposal which was agreed upon at the Vienna conference. Article 42(4) of Fitzmaurice's 'First Report on the Law of Treaties' stated that:

> Nevertheless, prior to its entry into force, a treaty has an operative effect . . . so far as concerns those of its provisions that regulate the processes of ratification, acceptance and similar matters, and the date or manner of entry into force itself . . .[48]

In his commentary Fitzmaurice justified this provision as follows:

> Logically, a treaty which, *ex hypothesi*, is not yet in force, cannot provide for its own entry into force—since, until that occurs, the clause so providing can itself have no force. The real truth is that, by a tacit assumption invariably made, the clauses of a treaty providing for ratification, accession, entry into force, and certain other possible matters, are deemed to come into force separately and at once, on signature—or are treated as if they did—even though the substance of the treaty does not.[49]

---

[48] A/CN.4/101 (14 March 1956), p. 42.

[49] *Loc. cit.*, p. 75.

The International Law Commission had not included any provision on this aspect of entry into force in the proposals which they had submitted in 1966. Accordingly, at the first session of the Vienna conference the United Kingdom delegation put forward a proposal based on the Fitzmaurice text. This received general support as a useful addition to the Commission text and was in principle accepted subject to redrafting by the Drafting Committee. Paragraph 4 of Article 24 of the Convention accordingly now specifies that 'the provisions of a treaty regulating the authentication of its text, the establishment of the consent of States to be bound by the treaty, the manner or date of its entry into force, reservations, the functions of the depositary, and other matters arising necessarily before the entry into force of the treaty apply from the time of the adoption of its text'.

The word 'necessarily' as used in this paragraph may not be entirely apposite. Certain of the listed matters, such as those concerning the establishment of the consent of States to be bound by a treaty, reservations and the functions of the depositary, may apply both before and after entry into force. 'Necessarily' should not accordingly be construed as meaning 'exclusively'; the concept is rather that there may be treaty provisions regulating other matters which may also arise before entry into force—for example, a clause providing for provisional application.

Article 25 of the Convention in fact deals with provisional application. Neither the Harvard draft nor McNair refer in terms to provisional application of a treaty. The inclusion in treaties of clauses providing for the provisional application of the whole or part of the treaty is a relatively recent development in international practice. It has been brought about principally because there may on occasions be an urgent need to realise immediate international co-operation on certain problems.[50]

The Commission had refrained from proposing any rule regarding the termination of provisional application of a treaty, stating that this point should be left to be determined by the agreement of the

[50] A good example is provided by the O.E.E.C. Convention, designed to give effect to the Marshall plan for economic co-operation in Europe in 1948. Given the urgency of the problems to be overcome, Article 24(b) of the Convention recorded the agreement of the signatories 'to put it into operation on signature on a provisional basis and in accordance with their several constitutional requirements'; see Treaty Series No. 59 (1949); Cmnd. 7796.

parties and the operation of the rules regarding termination of treaties.[51] The conference thought otherwise, however, and, on the basis of proposals by Belgium and by Hungary and Poland, adopted what is now paragraph 2 of Article 25, providing that the provisional application of a treaty with respect to a State is terminated if that State notifies the other States between which the treaty is being applied provisionally of its intention not to become a party.

The text of Article 25 is not, however, without difficulty. In the first place, there are instances in international practice where a treaty may continue to apply provisionally among certain States notwithstanding that it has entered into force definitively between other States. A statement by the United Kingdom delegation expressing the understanding that 'the inclusion of the phrase "pending its entry into force" in paragraph 1 did not preclude the provisional application of a treaty by one or more States after the treaty had entered into force definitively between other States' encountered no objection at the conference, and was indeed specifically endorsed by India.[52] In the second place, there are other instances where some only of the negotiating States may agree to apply the treaty or part of it provisionally pending its entry into force. Again, a statement by the United Kingdom delegation to the effect that 'paragraph 1(b) of [Article 25] would apply equally to the situation where certain of the negotiating States had agreed to apply the treaty or part of the treaty provisionally pending its entry into force' encountered no opposition at the conference and was specifically endorsed by India and Greece.[53]

[51] 1966 I.L.C. Reports, p. 42.

[52] *Official Records, Second Session,* 11th plenary meeting.

[53] *Loc. cit.*, statements by Sir Francis Vallat (U.K.), Jagota (India) and Eustathiades (Greece).

CHAPTER III

THE APPLICATION, INTERPRETATION AMENDMENT AND MODIFICATION OF TREATIES

Parts III and IV of the Vienna Convention cover the observance, application and interpretation of treaties and the amendment and modification of treaties respectively. Part III is divided into four sections headed observance of treaties, application of treaties, interpretation of treaties and treaties and third states. Part IV consists of three articles (Articles 39 to 41) under the heading amendment and modification of treaties. I propose to discuss the more important issues which arise under each of these headings.

I OBSERVANCE OF TREATIES

Article 26 of the Convention reproduces, in lapidary language, the basic principle *pacta sunt servanda*, designated by the Commission as 'the fundamental principle of the law of treaties'.[1] The Commission's formulation of the principle:

> Every treaty in force is binding upon the parties to it and must be performed by them in good faith

was adopted by the conference without change, although a group of States proposed to replace the words 'every treaty in force' by 'every *valid* treaty'. This was objected to, however, by other delegations on the grounds that it would weaken the text, that questions of validity were governed by Part V of the Convention and that, in any event, a treaty duly determined to be invalid would not be 'in force' for the purpose of the application of the rule. In the event, the amendment was not pressed to a vote, but was referred to the Drafting Committee, which reported out the original Commission text without change, the sponsors of the amendment making statements to the effect that the expression 'treaty in force' meant a treaty

[1] 1966 I.L.C. Reports, p. 42.

that was in force in accordance with the provisions of the Convention, including the provisions relating to validity.[2]

The genesis of what is now Article 27 of the Convention is to be found in an amendment tabled by Pakistan at the first session of the conference.[3] The Pakistan delegation wished it to be made clear that no party to a treaty might invoke the provisions of its constitution or its laws as an excuse for its failure to perform a treaty. The Pakistan amendment found general favour among delegations. It was explained that the Commission had not included this principle in its draft articles since it was thought that it belonged to the topic of State responsibility, although it had some relevance to the law of treaties.[4] The Pakistan amendment was nonetheless approved in principle and referred to the Drafting Committee. It was reported out with the addition of a qualification to the effect that the rule is without prejudice to Article 46. Article 46, of course, establishes that a State may not invoke the fact that its consent to be bound by a treaty has been expressed in violation of a provision of its internal law regarding competence to conclude treaties as invalidating its consent unless that violation was manifest and concerned a rule of its internal law of fundamental importance. Given the existence of the possible exception in Article 46 concerning manifest violations, it was not unnatural that the Drafting Committee should take the view that some qualification was necessary in Article 27, since 'there might be a certain overlapping between the two articles'.[5]

II APPLICATION OF TREATIES

Articles 28–30 of the Convention deal with three separate aspects of the application of treaties—application *ratione temporis*, application to territory and application of successive treaties relating to the same subject-matter.

I APPLICATION 'RATIONE TEMPORIS'

The Convention lays down the basic rule of non-retroactivity of treaties—that is to say that, unless a different intention appears from

[2] See statements by the delegations of Cyprus, Ecuador, Czechoslovakia, Bolivia and Spain in *Official Records, First Session,* 72nd meeting.

[3] A/Conf. 39/C.1/L.181.

[4] *Official Records, First Session,* 12th meeting (Sir Humphrey Waldock).

[5] *Official Records, First Session,* 72nd meeting, para. 32 (Yasseen).

the treaty or is otherwise established, its provisions do not bind a party in relation to any act or fact which took place or any situation which ceased to exist before the date of entry into force of the treaty with respect to that party. The basic rule of non-retroactivity is supported by the judgment of the International Court in the 'Ambatielos' case (Preliminary Objection), where the Court rejected a Greek contention that it was entitled, under a treaty of 1926, to present a claim based on acts which had taken place in 1922 and 1923 on the ground that this would mean giving retroactive effect to the 1926 treaty.[6]

It may be noted that the Convention itself embodies two other provisions which might, at first sight, be thought to derogate from the rule of non-retroactivity. There is first of all the rule laid down in Article 18 of the Convention (which we have already discussed) about the obligation of States not to defeat the object and purpose of a treaty prior to its entry into force. But it seems clear that the rule laid down in Article 18 is not a true exception to the principle of non-retroactivity. It is rather an expression of what is an autonomous obligation imposed upon States by virtue of the principle of good faith, quite independently of the treaty.[7] Second, there is the rule contained in Article 24(4) about the application of certain provisions of a treaty, such as those concerning authentication of the text and the manner and date of entry into force, from the time of the adoption of the text. This may be taken to be an example of a case where a different intention appears from the treaty, since the *rationale* of the rule expressed in Article 24(4) is the tacit assumption of the parties to a treaty that its formal provisions will become operative as from the adoption of the text so far as necessary to make those provisions effective.

I would draw attention to one final point. In the absence of any express provision in the Vienna Convention, Article 28 would have operated with respect to the Convention itself. But this was a cause of concern to many delegations, who were preoccupied with the possible application of a clause providing for compulsory settlement of disputes procedures to disputes arising in connection with treaties

[6] *I.C.J. Reports* (1952), p. 40.

[7] Cf. the explanation given by the chairman of the Drafting Committee for the refusal of the Drafting Commttee to accept a Finnish amendment proposing that a cross-reference to Article 18 be included in the text of what is now Article 28: *Official Records, First Session,* 72nd meeting (Yasseen).

concluded before the entry into force of the Vienna Convention. Accordingly, Article 4 of the Convention lays down a specific rule to the effect that, without prejudice to the application of customary rules, the Convention applies only to treaties concluded by States after the entry into force of the Convention with regard to such States.

2 APPLICATION TO TERRITORY

More difficult doctrinally, and indeed in terms of practice, is the question of the territorial application of treaties. One has to start from the proposition that not all treaties apply territorially. Some treaties apply exclusively to the State as an international person, that is to say, they apply *ratione personae*. Examples of such treaties are treaties of alliance, treaties establishing international organisations and treaties for the submission of a dispute to arbitration or adjudication. It is obvious that treaties of this nature are intended to bind the States parties as political entities and not in respect of a particular stretch of territory. There are other treaties which apply to the nationals of a State, whether within the national territory or not. Such treaties, if they purport to establish rights and obligations for nationals, irrespective of their place of residence or domicile, may not have any clear territorial application; but treaties of this nature may of course be of a mixed character—for example, a visa abolition agreement will accord rights to the nationals of the parties but will also have a specified territorial application.

But let us confine ourselves to those treaties which unquestionably do apply territorially. What is the rule of international law which applies when the treaty is silent on its territorial application? Doctrine has been divided on this point, particularly on the question whether a 'silent' treaty applies only to the metropolitan territory of the State or to both metropolitan and non-metropolitan territories. This is clearly a matter of prime importance to those States, such as the United Kingdom, which possess both metropolitan and overseas territories and bear a measure of international responsibility for the conduct of the international relations of other territories with whom they are in treaty relations. The nature of the problem is perhaps best described in the following extract from a statement prepared by the Secretariat of the United Nations in 1952:

Thus, although, from the international point of view, the United Kingdom is responsible for its overseas territories, and can conclude treaties which apply to those territories, the constitutional relationship of the territories to the United Kingdom varies widely according to the status of the territory concerned. Because of the intricate legal issues which may arise in connection with the application to any such territory of a treaty concluded by the United Kingdom the latter has, for many years, made a practice of ensuring the insertion in its treaties of an article (the so-called 'colonial' article) providing, either that the treaty applies to territories 'for whose international relations the United Kingdom is responsible' if special notice to that effect is given (thus implying that, in the absence of any such notice, it extends to the metropolitan territory only) or, in the reverse form, under which the territories are included unless a declaration is made, or notice given, that the treaty shall not apply to specified territories in the absence of a special acceptance on their behalf.[8]

It should be noted that this is a description of the situation as it existed in 1952. I will not seek to describe subsequent developments in any detail. It is sufficient to note that the so-called 'colonial' article, whether in the contracting-in or in the contracting-out version, has come under increasing attack within the framework of conferences organised by, or under the auspices of, the United Nations on the grounds that it accords recognition to, or seeks to perpetuate, colonial-type situations which should be brought to an end with all reasonable despatch. This opposition to the inclusion in general multilateral treaties concluded under the auspices of the United Nations of clauses relating to territorial application has led to a marked increase in the number of such treaties which are 'silent' on territorial application, thereby posing in stark fashion the problem of what is the residual rule.

As I have indicated earlier, doctrine is somewhat divided on this point. McNair expresses the predominant trend of opinion when he states:

> The treaty may be of such a kind that it contains no obvious restriction of its application to any particular geographical area . . . in such a case the rule is that, subject to express or implied provision to the contrary, the treaty applies to all the territory of the Contracting Party, whether metropolitan or not.[9]

[8] *Laws and Practices concerning the Conclusion of Treaties,* United Nations Legislative Series, 1953 (ST/LEG/Ser.B/3), pp. 122–3.

[9] *Op. cit.,* pp. 116–17. To the same effect, see Fawcett, *The British Commonwealth in International Law* (1963), pp. 210–14, and Higgins, *The Development of International Law by the Political Organs of the United Nations* (1963), p. 310.

Several Continental jurists have, however, taken the opposite view —that, in principle, a 'silent' treaty applies exclusively to the metropolitan territory of a State and does not affect dependent territories. Thus Rousseau states the basic rule as follows:

> Réserve faite de l'hypothèse où, par son objet, un traité concerne exclusivement des colonies, les traités conclus par un Etat ne s'étendent pas de plein droit à ses colonies.[10]

Others again have expressed themselves more cautiously to the effect that the applicability of treaties to overseas possessions or other dependent territories is doubtful and depends from case to case on the basic intention of the parties.[11]

The practice of the United Kingdom tends in the direction indicated by McNair. Arguing in favour of the inclusion in a United Nations Convention of a suitable territorial application article, the then Minister of State for Foreign Affairs (Mr Godber) drew the attention of the General Assembly in 1962 to the fact that most United Kingdom dependent territories were in large measure self-governing; he went on to say that 'if there is no such provision, it really means that all the people living in those territories, including the British Isles itself, will be excluded [from the Convention] until the last one is in a position to accept.'[12] Implied support for the McNair view can also be deduced from the statement made by the United Kingdom representative to the United Nations Commission on the Status of Women in 1963 to the effect that the United Kingdom government 'could not ratify the Convention on Political Rights of Women because it had no territorial application clause and some territories would be unable to conform to the Convention'.[13]

So matters stood before the Vienna Convention. The Commission, in their final set of draft articles, proposed a simple clause to the effect that 'unless a different intention appears from the treaty or is otherwise established, the application of a treaty extends to the entire territory of each party'. The proposed rule was justified on the basis that 'State practice, the jurisprudence of international

[10] *Principes Généraux du droit international public*, vol. I (1944), p. 381. In the same sense, Huber, *Le Droit de conclure des traités internationaux* (1951), p. 28.

[11] Dahm, *Völkerrecht*, vol. 3 (1961), p. 110.

[12] Cited in *British Practice in International Law* (1962—II), p. 237.

[13] Cited in *British Practice in International Law* (1963—II), p. 144.

tribunals and the writings of jurists appear to support the view that a treaty is to be presumed to apply to all the territory of each party unless it otherwise appears from the treaty'.[14]

The Commission likewise stated in their commentary that they preferred the phrase 'the entire territory of each party' to the phrase 'all the territory or territories for which the parties are internationally responsible' because of the association of the latter term with the so-called 'colonial' clause. The phrase 'the entire territory of each party' was intended to be a comprehensive term designed to embrace all the land and appurtenant territorial waters and air space which constitute the territory of the State.[15]

There was little discussion of this provision at the Vienna conference. Following upon an amendment tabled by the Ukraine, the drafting of the article was slightly modified to take account of a problem concerning the relationship of international law to internal law. The Australian delegation, having surveyed the problems confronting States parts of whose territories were regarded as distinct for the purposes of various phases of the treaty-making process, concluded that '[Article 29] was only a residual rule of interpretation and could not in any way be construed as a norm requiring a State to express its consent to be bound by treaties without first establishing whether the treaty was acceptable and applicable to all the component parts of the State'.[16] The United Kingdom delegation stated, in a brief intervention, their understanding that 'the expression "its entire territory" applied solely to the territory over which a party to the treaty in question exercised its sovereignty'.[17]

It is clear that the opening words of Article 29 of the Convention impart a considerable degree of flexibility into the operation of the basic rule. But in what circumstances will a different intention appear from the treaty or be otherwise established? In other words, what exceptions are there to the residual rule?

It would appear that exceptions to the residual rule can be either express or implied. The obvious express exception is a territorial application clause in the treaty itself. But there can be other kinds of express exception. The device whereby, on signature or ratifica-

[14] 1966 I.L.C. Reports, p. 45.
[15] *Ibid.*
[16] *Official Records, First Session,* 30th meeting (Harry).
[17] *Loc. cit.,* 72nd meeting (Sinclair).

tion, a State makes a declaration as to the territorial effect or extent of the act of signature or ratification has long been known and accepted in State practice. Thus, in ratifying the Convention on the High Seas in 1963, the United Kingdom government declared that 'ratification of this Convention on behalf of the United Kingdom does not extend to the States in the Persian Gulf enjoying British protection'.[18] So also, in signing the European Convention on the International Classification of Patents for Invention, the United Kingdom signatory declared 'that my signature is in respect of the United Kingdom of Great Britain and Northern Ireland (including the Isle of Man) and is not in respect of any other territory or territories for whose international relations the Government of the United Kingdom are responsible'.[19] Numerous other examples of comparable declarations, made on signature or on ratification, could be cited. The recent practice of the United Kingdom in relation to treaties which are 'silent' on territorial application appears to be to specify in the instrument of ratification itself the territories in respect of which the treaty is being ratified. Thus, ratification by the United Kingdom of the Treaty on the Non-proliferation of Nuclear Weapons is in respect of the United Kingdom of Great Britain and Northern Ireland, the Associated States (Antigua, Dominica, Grenada, Saint Christopher–Nevis–Anguilla and Saint Lucia) and territories under the territorial sovereignty of the United Kingdom, as well as the State of Brunei, the kingdom of Tonga and the British Solomon Islands protectorate.[20]

Another category of express exception to the residual rule would be a reservation on territorial application duly established *vis-à-vis* the other parties to the treaty in question. Examples of such reservations are not infrequent in practice, and they may, of course, be combined with declarations of the kind indicated above. Thus, on acceding to the Convention on Consent to Marriage, Minimum Age for Marriage and Registration of Marriage in 1970, the United Kingdom instrument of accession specified, as for the Non-

[18] Treaty Series, No. 5 (1963): Cmnd. 1929.

[19] Treaty Series, No. 12 (1963): Cmnd. 1956.

[20] Treaty Series, No. 88 (1970). The U.K. instrument of ratification of the Treaty on Principles Governing the Activities of States in the Exploration and Use of Outer Space, including the Moon and Other Celestial Bodies, similarly defines the territories in respect of which the treaty is being ratified; see Treaty Series, No. 10 (1968): Cmnd. 3519.

proliferation Treaty, the territories in respect of which the accession took effect; but it was accompanied by a reservation postponing the application of Article 2 of the Convention in Montserrat pending notification to the Secretary-General that the article will be applied there.[21]

A word of caution is, however, necessary here. A reservation on the territorial application of certain types of treaty may be excluded because such a reservation would be incompatible with the object and purpose of the treaty. There are certain treaties, principally in the field of disarmament or humanitarian law, which are clearly intended to be world-wide in their application. It is arguable that the nature of such treaties would preclude the making of a reservation designed to limit their territorial application.

I have so far concentrated on express provisions operating as exceptions to the residual rule. What about implied exceptions? The principal implied exception is a treaty adopted by, or within the framework of, a regional organisation or intended to apply only within a particular region. Where such a treaty is 'silent' as to its territorial application, its regional character may be such as to create a presumption that territorial units outside the region which are dependent upon a State within the region are excluded. Thus the United Kingdom government ratified the Agreement on Travel by Young Persons on Collective Passports between Member Countries of the Council of Europe (an agreement adopted within the framework of the Council of Europe but containing no express provision on territorial application) 'in respect of the United Kingdom of Great Britain and Northern Ireland, Jersey, the Bailiwick of Guernsey, the Isle of Man, Gibraltar and the State of Malta only'.[22]

The context of a particular treaty can also constitute an implied exception to the residual rule. An example would be a treaty which specified a particular zone of application (thereby impliedly excluding any dependent territories not included within the zone).

Thus it would appear that the operation of the residual rule on territorial application is subject to a number of exceptions. In cases where a particular treaty is silent upon its territorial application, declarations made by a State on signature or ratification, the specific terms of an instrument of ratification or accession or a valid reserva-

[21] Treaty Series, No. 102 (1970): Cmnd. 4538.
[22] Treaty Series, No. 52 (1964): Cmnd. 2482.

tion can operate to exclude the rule. Furthermore, the regional character, or the particular context, of a treaty may impliedly operate to exclude the rule, in so far as the regional character or context is indicative of the intention of the parties that the treaty should have a limited territorial application.

3 APPLICATION OF SUCCESSIVE TREATIES RELATING TO THE SAME SUBJECT-MATTER

A particularly obscure aspect of the law of treaties is the question of application of successive treaties which relate to the same subject-matter. With the post-war growth in international co-operation, accompanied by a massive increase in the numbers and range of international agreements of a law-making character, the problem of incidental conflict between successive treaties has become more acute. This is in part attributable to the very nature of the international legislative process, characterised as it is by a diversity of functional or regional organisations having overlapping responsibilities for the preparation of international Conventions for acceptance by States.[23]

McNair discusses this question of incompatible treaties in some detail. He deals first with the situation where the treaties which are alleged to be in conflict are made by the same parties on different dates. In these circumstances, and as a matter of interpretation, the later treaty will prevail:

> Where the parties to the two treaties said to be in conflict are the same, an allegation of conflict raises a question of interpretation rather than a question of a rule of law; the parties are masters of the situation and they are free to modify one treaty by a later one.[24]

Where the earlier treaty is general in nature and the later treaty contains special and detailed rules, the operation of the maxim *generalia specialibus non derogant* would in any event ensure that the later treaty prevailed.

The complications begin when the case is one of conflict between a treaty to which States A and B are parties and a later treaty to

[23] Jenks, 'The conflict of law-making treaties' in 30 *B.Y.I.L.* (1953), pp. 401–453.

[24] *Op. cit.*, p. 219.

which States A and C are parties. McNair suggests four cases in which the later treaty may be null and void:

(*a*) Where, by virtue of the earlier treaty, State A has surrendered or diminished its treaty-making capacity and the later treaty has been concluded by State A in the absence, or in excess, of its treaty-making capacity.
(*b*) Where the earlier treaty is of a constitutive character (such as the Charter of the United Nations) and State A later concludes a treaty which is in conflict with an imperative provision of the earlier treaty.
(*c*) If the earlier treaty is a multipartite law-making treaty clearly intended to create permanent rules and containing no power of denunciation, and the later treaty purports to derogate from its provisions.
(*d*) If the performance of the second treaty involves a violation of 'universal law'.[25]

McNair then goes on to maintain that, in other cases, the later treaty will not be void. State A, in the hypothetical situation envisaged, would not *ipso facto* be committing a wrongful act against State B by concluding a later, inconsistent treaty with State C. State A would commit a wrongful act against State B only by failing to perform its treaty with State B; and if State A fails to perform its later treaty with State C, it would incur responsibility towards the latter, provided at any rate that State C had been unaware of the earlier treaty between States A and B.[26]

The Commission were clearly puzzled as to how to deal with this complex problem on the borderline between the law of treaties and the law relating to State responsibility. Lauterpacht, in his 'First Report on the Law of Treaties', suggested the general rule that a treaty is void if its performance involves a breach of a treaty obligation previously undertaken by one or more of the contracting parties.[27] Fitzmaurice took a position closer to that outlined by McNair. Where a treaty between State A and C was inconsistent with an earlier treaty between States A and B, the second treaty was not to be invalid, but State A might incur responsibility to either State B or State C for failure to perform its treaty obligations. The

[25] *Op. cit.*, p. 221.
[26] *Op. cit.*, pp. 221–2.
[27] A/CN.4/63 (1953), Article 16(1).

later treaty would be invalid only when (*a*) the earlier treaty had expressly prohibited the conclusion of a later inconsistent treaty or (*b*) the later treaty necessarily involved a direct breach of the earlier treaty.[28]

Waldock reviewed *de novo* the proposals of the previous Special Rapporteurs and recommended that the approach based on the invalidity of a later, inconsistent treaty be dropped. He did not feel that the 'Oscar Chinn'[29] case or the 'European Commission of the Danube'[30] case afforded real support for the doctrine of the invalidity of a later treaty which infringes the rights of third States under a prior treaty. He was rather of the view that the issue should be approached, not from the point of view of the validity or invalidity of the later treaty, but from that of the *priority* of incompatible treaty obligations.[31]

The Convention regime on successive treaties, which is based largely on Waldock's proposals, may be briefly summarised as follows:

(*a*) If a treaty says that it is subject to, or is not to be considered as incompatible with, another treaty, that other treaty will prevail.

(*b*) As between parties to a treaty who become parties to a later, inconsistent, treaty, the earlier treaty will apply only where its provisions are not incompatible with the later treaty.

(*c*) As between a party to both treaties and a party to only one of them, the treaty to which both are parties will govern the mutual rights and obligations of the States concerned.

These rules are expressed to be without prejudice to the rules governing the *inter se* modification of multilateral treaties by certain of the

[28] Fitzmaurice, 'Third Report on the Law of Treaties', A/CN.4/115 (1958), Articles 18 and 19.

[29] P.C.I.J., Series A/B, No. 63. In this case Judges Van Eysinga and Schücking, in dissenting judgments, had asserted the invalidity of the Convention of St Germain, a later treaty between certain of the parties to the General Act of Berlin of 1885, which purported to modify the latter. But the Court were content to regard the Convention of St Germain, which had been relied on by both the litigating States as the source of their obligations, as the treaty which must be applied.

[30] P.C.I.J., Series B, No. 14.

[31] Waldock, 'Second Report on the Law of Treaties', A/CN.4/156 (1963), pp. 53–72.

parties only, or to any question of termination or suspension of the operation of a treaty as a consequence of its breach, or to any question of responsibility which may arise for a State from the conclusion or application of a treaty which is incompatible with its obligations towards another State under another treaty.

Although these rules may appear to be somewhat complicated, their substance is relatively simple. Indeed, it is their very simplicity which may occasion some concern, given the varying types of situation which they are designed to cover. A particular problem arises, for example, with respect to 'chains' of treaties where, for eminently practical reasons, it may be necessary to apply the later treaty even *vis-à-vis* States which are parties only to the earlier treaty. The rules and practices of B.I.R.P.I. (International Bureaux for the Protection of Intellectual and Industrial Property) afford an example of the kind of problem which can arise. The observer from the Bureau explained the difficulty at the conference in the following terms:

> However, a special situation existed in international Unions such as those administered by B.I.R.P.I., which included the Unions instituted by the 1883 Paris Convention for the Protection of Industrial Property and the 1886 Berne Convention for the Protection of Literary and Artistic Works. Those Conventions had been revised on several occasions but each revision was merely a different version of the original Convention, which continued to exist. There was only one Union constituted by each original Convention.
>
> Technically, each original Convention and its revising Acts were separate and successive treaties, each calling for ratification. A State, however, sometimes acceded to the most recent Act of a Union, without declaring that its accession was valid for the previous Acts. In its relations with States parties to the most recent Act, no problem arose. In its relations with States members of the Union but not parties to the most recent Act, on the other hand, the acceding State was understood to have tacitly accepted all the previous texts, so that its relations with the States parties only to the earlier texts were governed by those earlier texts. The legal position was arguable, but the system was the only practicable one. The Union was more important than the Convention which had set it up. Without that tacit acceptance system, the State acceding to the latest text would have no relations with half the membership of the Union.[32]

[32] *Official Records, First Session,* 31st meeting (Woodley). But it should be noted that Article 32(2) of the (latest) Stockholm revision of the Berne Convention requires countries outside the Union which become parties to the

The special features of the system operating within the framework of the Berne and Paris Union are fortunately preserved by the saving clause in Article 5 of the Vienna Convention, which protects 'any relevant rules' of an international organisation. These rules embrace not only written rules but also 'unwritten customary rules'.[33] But it is not to be thought that the B.I.R.P.I. system constitutes a unique exception to the general rules. Other international organisations of a technical character also operate rules which differ from those laid down in Article 30. Thus the Universal Postal Union and the International Telecommunications Union have been accustomed to re-enact their basic constitutional instruments every five years. This has involved the abrogation of the existing Convention and its replacement by a new Convention. But complications have arisen because of the failure of some member countries of the Union to ratify the new Convention by the date of its entry into force, which is always a fixed date. Rules and practices have therefore been developed whereby States which, for one reason or another, have failed to ratify a revised postal Convention continue to participate in the world postal regime on the basis of tacit adherence to the Convention.[34] Similar, but more formal, arrangements apply within the International Telecommunications Union.[35]

Because of the inevitable complications surrounding this question of incompatibility between successive treaties relating to the same subject-matter, it may be useful to draw attention to certain points of clarification which emerge from a study of the conference records.

First, and perhaps most important, it is clear that the rules laid down in Article 30 are intended to be residuary rules—that is to say, rules which will operate in the absence of express treaty provisions regulating priority. Paragraph 2 of the commentary to

---

Stockholm Act to apply it with respect to any country of the Union which is not a party to the Stockholm Act. But, in the converse case, the country of the Union which is not a party to the Stockholm Act is entitled to apply the provisions of the most recent Act to which it is a party and to adapt the protection to the level provided for by Stockholm; see Treaty Series, No. 53 (1970): Cmnd. 4412.

[33] *Official Records, First Session,* 28th meeting (explanation given by Yasseen, chairman of the Drafting Committee).

[34] Alexandrowicz, *World Economic Agencies* (1962), p. 16.

[35] *Ibid.*, pp. 40–1.

the proposal submitted by the Commission had already drawn attention to the fact that 'treaties not infrequently contain a clause intended to regulate the relation between the provisions of the treaty and those of another treaty or of any other treaty related to the matters with which the treaty deals' and that 'whatever the nature of the provision, the clause has necessarily to be taken into account in appreciating the priority of successive treaties relating to the same subject matter'.[36] But the Commission's proposal was not (and indeed the text of Article 30 is not) drafted in such a way as to make it clear that the proposed rules were residuary in nature. However, in response to a comment made at the conference, Sir Humphrey Waldock confirmed 'that the rules in paragraphs 3, 4 and 5 were thus designed essentially as residuary rules'.[37]

Second, the chairman of the Drafting Committee, in introducing the revised text of what later became Article 30 at the 91st meeting of the Committee of the Whole, clarified the meaning to be attached to the concept of compatibility as used in paragraph 3 of the Article. Ambassador Yasseen spoke as follows:

> In the view of the Drafting Committee, the mere fact that there was a difference between the provisions of a later treaty and those of an earlier treaty did not necessarily mean that there existed an incompatibility within the meaning of the last phrase of paragraph 3. In point of fact, maintenance in force of the provisions of the earlier treaty might be justified by circumstances or by the intention of the parties. That would be so, for example, in the following case. If a small number of States concluded a consular convention granting wide privileges and immunities, and those same States later concluded with other States a consular convention having a much larger number of parties but providing for a more restricted regime, the earlier convention would continue to govern relations between the States parties thereto if the circumstances or the intention of the parties justified its maintenance in force.[38]

This is clearly relevant to the type of problem which arises when there coexist two international Conventions on the same subject-matter, one adopted within a regional framework and one within a universal framework. A good example is afforded by the European Convention on Human Rights and the United Nations Covenants on Human Rights. Quite apart from any conflict of substantive

[36] 1966 I.L.C. Reports, p. 46.
[37] *Official Records, Second Session,* 91st meeting.
[38] *Ibid.*

provisions, there would inevitably, unless special provision had been made, have been a conflict between the implementation provisions of the two Conventions. For this reason, Article 44 of the United Nations Covenant on Civil and Political Rights states that

> the provisions for the implementation of the present Covenant shall apply without prejudice to the procedures prescribed in the field of human rights by or under the consituient instruments and the conventions of the United Nations and of the specialised agencies and shall not prevent the States Parties to the present Covenant from having recourse to other procedures for settling a dispute in accordance with general or special international agreements in force between them.[39]

Third, it seems clear that, in determining which treaty is the 'earlier' and which the 'later', the relevant date is that of the adoption of the text and not that of its entry into force. Adoption of the second treaty manifests the new legislative intent.[40] But, of course, the rules laid down in Article 30 have effect for each individual party to a treaty only as from the date of entry into force of the treaty for that party.

Finally, it would seem that the expression 'relating to the same subject-matter' must be construed strictly. It will not cover cases where a general treaty impinges indirectly on the content of a particular provision of an earlier treaty. Accordingly, a general treaty on the reciprocal enforcement of judgments will not affect the continued applicability of particular provisions concerning the enforcement of judgments contained in an earlier treaty dealing with third-party liability in the field of nuclear energy. This is not a question of the application of successive treaties relating to the same subject-matter, but is rather a question of treaty interpretation

[39] Miscellaneous No. 4 (1967): Cmnd. 3220 (Article 44). But Article 44 of the United Nations Covenant by no means resolves all the problems of potential conflict between the European and United Nations Conventions; see Eissen, 'Convention Européenne des Droits de l'Homme et Pacte des Nations Unies relatifs aux droits civils et politiques: problèmes de coexistence', 30 *Zeitschrift für ausländisches öffentliches Recht und Völkerrecht* (1970), pp. 237–61 and 646–7, and Robertson, *Human Rights in the World* (1972), pp. 80–110. For a brief discussion of the interaction between the Vienna Convention on Consular Relations and the European Convention on Consular Functions, see Maryan Green in 8 *Revue Belge de Droit International* (1972), p. 184.

[40] *Official Records, Second Session,* 91st meeting (Waldock). If the rule were otherwise, there could be serious complications: see *Official Records, First Session,* 31st meeting (Sinclair).

involving consideration of the maxim *generalia specialibus non derogant*.[41]

It will be apparent from this brief analysis that Article 30 of the Vienna Convention is in many respects not entirely satisfactory. The rules laid down fail to take account of the many complications which arise when there coexist two treaties relating to the same subject-matter, one negotiated at the regional level among States between whom there is a high degree of mutual confidence and another negotiated within the framework of a universal organisation. The complications are perhaps such that no attempt to lay down general rules would have disposed of all the difficulties; this is an area where State practice is continually developing, and where it may possibly have been premature to seek to establish fixed guidelines. Perhaps little harm has been done so long as the Convention rules are regarded as residuary in character, so that the negotiators of treaties are left reasonably free to determine for themselves the relationship between the text which they are seeking to draw up and previous, or future, treaties in the same field.

III INTERPRETATION OF TREATIES

There are few topics in international law which have given rise to such extensive doctrinal dispute as the topic of treaty interpretation. The passion which is generated among jurists on this one issue is such that, with McNair, your lecturer confesses that 'there is no part of the law of treaties which [he] approaches with more trepidation than the question of interpretation'.[42]

Let us begin by seeking to analyse what are the main areas of contention. At one end of the spectrum, there are those who in essence deny the existence of any rules or principles governing treaty interpretation, arguing that their application in any particular case is merely an *ex post facto* rationalisation of a conclusion reached on other grounds or serves as a cover for judicial creativeness.[43] This somewhat extreme view is understandable as a reaction against the indiscriminate use of the hotchpotch of contradictory and conflicting

[41] *Official Records, Second Session*, 85th meeting (Sinclair) and 91st meeting (Waldock).

[42] *Op. cit.*, p. 364.

[43] See, for example, Stone, 'Fictional elements in treaty interpretation', 1 *Sydney Law Review* (1955), pp. 344–68.

maxims asserted by certain writers to constitute the applicable principles of treaty interpretation; but it gives no constructive guidance as to the attitude which an international tribunal will take when confronted with a problem of treaty interpretation, and it ignores the *indicia* (unhelpful and conflicting though they may be) which are available as a guide to what that attitude is likely to be.

At the other end of the spectrum will be found those who, far from wishing the would-be interpreter to traverse the arid desert without signposts, seek to plunge him into the impenetrable jungle of interpretation by reference to 'overriding community goals' while instructing him not to ignore any pathway (however meandering) which might be thought to lead in the direction of the 'genuine shared expectations' of the parties.[44]

But, first, you may ask, what is the aim and goal of treaty interpretation? Even on this preliminary issue, there is a measure of disagreement among publicists. On the one hand, there are those who assert that the primary, and indeed only, aim and goal of treaty interpretation is to ascertain the intention of the parties.[45] There are others who start from the proposition that there must exist a presumption that the intentions of the parties are reflected in the text of the treaty which they have drawn up, and that the primary goal of treaty interpretation is to ascertain the meaning of this text.[46] Finally, there are those who maintain that the decision-maker must first ascertain the object and purpose of a treaty and then interpret it so as to give effect to that object and purpose.[47]

These three different schools of thought, with their varying emphases, are commonly said to reflect the subjective (or 'intentions of the parties') approach, the objective (or 'textual') approach and the teleological (or 'object and purpose') approach.[48] They are not,

[44] McDougal, Lasswell and Miller, *Interpretation of Agreements and World Public Order* (1967). For a comprehensive critique of this approach, see Fitzmaurice, '*Vae victis*, or, Woe to the negotiators', 65 *A.J.I.L.* (1971), pp. 358–73.

[45] Verdross, *Völkerrecht*, fifth edition (1964), p. 173; *Parry in Manual of Public International Law*, ed. Sorensen (1968), p. 210; and, above all, Lauterpacht in *Annuaire de l'Institut de Droit International*, 43(1) (1950), pp. 366–434.

[46] Fitzmaurice in 33 *B.Y.I.L.* (1957), pp. 204–7.

[47] Article 19(a) of the Harvard draft reflects this approach.

[48] See Jacobs, 'Varieties of approach to treaty interpretation: with special reference to the draft Convention on the Law of Treaties before the Vienna diplomatic conference', 18 *I.C.L.Q.* (1969), pp. 318–46, and Sinclair, *loc. cit.*, p. 61.

of course, mutually exclusive. The most rigid adherent of the textual approach would scarcely argue that a tribunal should deliberately seek to establish a meaning which was not within the contemplation, or intention, of any of the parties to the dispute; and the most rigid adherent of the intentions approach would not seek to deny that the text of the treaty will constitute evidence of what was the intent of the parties.

McNair, in an attempt to find a synthesis of all three approaches, suggests that the main task of any tribunal which is called upon to construe or apply or interpret a treaty is to give effect to the expressed intention of the parties, that is 'their intention as expressed in the words used by them in the light of the surrounding circumstances.'[49]

The Commission, in their final set of draft articles, suggested a general rule of interpretation in the following terms: 'A treaty shall be interpreted in good faith in accordance with the ordinary meaning to be given to the terms of the treaty in their context and in the light of its object and purpose.' This was accompanied by a definition of what is meant by the context of the treaty and what other elements have to be taken into account together with the context—namely, any subsequent practice in the application of the treaty establishing the understanding of the parties regarding its interpretation, and any relevant rules of international law. The *travaux préparatoires* of a treaty, together with the circumstances of its conclusion, are characterised as 'supplementary means' of interpretation which may be resorted to to confirm the meaning resulting from the application of the general rule, or to determine the meaning when the interpretation according to the general rule leaves the meaning ambiguous or obscure or leads to a result which is manifestly absurd or unreasonable.

The Commission's proposals (which were adopted virtually without change by the conference and are now reflected in Articles 31 and 32 of the Convention) were clearly based on the view that the text of a treaty must be presumed to be the authentic expression of the intentions of the parties; the Commission accordingly came down firmly in favour of the view that 'the starting point of interpretation is the elucidation of the meaning of the text, not an investigation *ab initio* into the intentions of the parties'.[50] This is not

[49] *Op. cit.*, p. 365.
[50] 1966 I.L.C. Reports, p. 51.

to say that the *travaux préparatoires* of a treaty, or the circumstances of its conclusion, are relegated to a subordinate, and wholly ineffective, role. As Professor Briggs points out, no rigid temporal prohibition on resort to the *travaux préparatoires* of a treaty was intended by the use of the phrase 'supplementary means of interpretation' in what is now Article 32 of the Vienna Convention.[51] The distinction between the general rule of interpretation and the supplementary means of interpretation is intended rather to ensure that the supplementary means do not constitute an alternative, autonomous method of interpretation divorced from the general rule.

The question of recourse to *travaux préparatoires* has often been regarded as the touchstone which serves to distinguish the adherents of the 'textual' approach from the adherents of the 'intentions' approach. It is implied that those who attach prime significance to the text of a treaty are reluctant to countenance resort to the *travaux préparatoires*, which will afford useful evidence as to the intention of the parties.[52] But this is not necessarily so. If the intentions of the parties, or the object and purpose of a treaty, do not reveal themselves from a careful analysis of the text, it is unlikely that the *travaux* will shed a pellucid light upon the matter. And, even if they did, there would still remain a difference of approach; for, in the case of those who favour the 'textual' approach, resort to the *travaux préparatoires* is for the purpose of elucidating the meaning of the text, not for the purpose of ascertaining, independently of the text, the intentions of the parties.

In any event, it is clear that no would-be interpreter of a treaty, whatever his doctrinal point of departure, will deliberately ignore any material which can usefully serve as a guide towards establishing the meaning of the text with which he is confronted. It can readily be admitted that the famous principle laid down by Vattel—'La première maxime générale sur l'interprétation est qu'il n'est pas permis d'interpréter ce qui n'a pas besoin d'interprétation'—is a *petitio principii*. It is obvious that this states the result of a process of interpretation rather than a rule about interpretation itself. Every text, however clear on its face, requires to be scrutinised in its context and in the light of the object and purpose which it is designed to serve. The *conclusion* which may be reached after such

[51] 'The *travaux préparatoires* of the Vienna Convention on the Law of Treaties', 65 *A.J.I.L.* (1971), p. 709.

[52] *Annuaire de l'Institut de Droit International,* 43(1) (1950), p. 392.

a scrutiny is, in most instances, that the clear meaning which originally presented itself is the correct one, but this should not be used to disguise the fact that what is involved is a process of interpretation.

It is suggested that many of the doctrinal disputes about treaty interpretation are somewhat unreal. There are, no doubt, real differences of emphasis as to what is the proper aim and goal of treaty interpretation. These differences we have already discussed. But, for the rest, many of the features that are said to distinguish the adherents of one school from the adherents of another stem from the fact that the argument is being conducted on two different levels. On the one hand, there are those who are seeking, as it were, to *describe* the process of interpretation and who, accordingly, focus attention upon the materials which the would-be interpreter should consult; and, on the other hand, there are those who are seeking to establish certain principles or rules as to the relative value or weight to be attributed to the materials to be taken into consideration.

It must be said that the Convention rules on interpretation reflect an attempt to assess the relative value and weight of the elements to be taken into account in the process of interpretation rather than to describe the process of interpretation itself. This does *not* mean that the Convention system establishes a rigid and utterly unyielding hierarchy between the general rule and the supplementary means. The relationship is considerably more subtle than that. The would-be interpreter is still expected, when confronted with a problem of treaty interpretation (which, *ex hypothesi*, involves an argument as to the meaning of a text) to have recourse to all the materials which will furnish him with evidence as to what is the meaning to be attributed to the text; such materials will naturally include the *travaux préparatoires* of the treaty, and the circumstances of its conclusion. It is only when he has available to him all the necessary materials that he will be in a position to assess their relative value and weight in the light of the rules laid down in the Convention.

It has been argued that the Convention rules on treaty interpretation constitute a departure from the *lex lata* and can be justified only by reference to their value in preventing conflict.[53] This argument is difficult to sustain. It is based on the assumption that the only relevant rule of customary international law is that the meaning and

[53] Schwarzenberger, 'Myths and Realities of Treaty Interpretation' in *Current Legal Problems* (1969), pp. 205–27.

effect of consensual obligations must be interpreted in a spirit of equity. But this comes very near to an assertion that the principles which international tribunals purport to apply are no more than an exercise in justification, disguise and self-deception. This is no doubt one view of the matter (and it is a view to which we have already drawn attention) but it is not a view which commands general support.

More significantly, it is asserted that the Convention rules are incomplete and possibly misleading. Thus, O'Connell maintains that 'the priorities inherent in the application of these rules are not clearly indicated, and the rules themselves are in part so general that it is necessary to review traditional methods whenever interpreting a treaty'.[54] The criticism directed towards the generality of the rules is no doubt well founded if (but only if) the intention had been to formulate a comprehensive code of the canons of interpretation available to international tribunals or other decision-makers. But the Commission specifically disavowed any such intent in making the proposals which (with very minor drafting changes) now appear as Articles 31 and 32 of the Convention. In their commentary the Commission refer to the rich variety of principles and maxims of interpretation applied by international tribunals. They point out that these are, for the most part, principles of logic and good sense which are valuable only as guides to assist in appreciating the meaning which the parties may have intended to attach to the expressions employed in a document; and that recourse to many of these principles is discretionary rather than obligatory, interpretation being to some extent an art rather than an exact science. Accordingly, the Commission concluded that 'any attempt to codify the conditions of the application of those principles of interpretation whose appropriateness in any given case depends on the particular context and on a subjective appreciation of varying circumstances would clearly be inadvisable'.[55]

O'Connell also characterises the general rule laid down in the Convention as embodying the literal and teleological techniques of interpretation. He argues that the teleological technique is not altogether the same as the principle of effectiveness 'and the omission of any reference to the principle of effectiveness in Article 31 will lead States to argue that it is not an established canon of interpreta-

[54] *Op. cit.*, p. 253.
[55] 1966 I.L.C. Reports, p. 50.

tion'.[56] It is doubtful whether the wording of Article 31 could be invoked to sustain so narrow a view. Certainly, the Commission seem to have believed that the principle of effectiveness expressed in the maxim *ut res magis valeat quam pereat* was subsumed in the reference to 'good faith' and 'the object and purpose of a treaty' contained in Article 31:

When a treaty is open to two interpretations one of which does and the other does not enable the treaty to have appropriate effects, good faith and the objects and purpose of the treaty demand that the former interpretation should be adopted.[57]

It may be that the teleological approach differs in some respects from the approach based on effectiveness, since it can be argued that the effective interpretation of a treaty is a matter of necessity based upon the presumed interest of the authors to make the treaty provision effective rather than ineffective, whereas interpretation by reference to the object and purpose of a treaty requires a subjective appreciation by the would-be interpreter of what were the aims of the parties.[58] The criticism is a fair one, but it would appear from the Commission's commentary that, in their view, the object and purpose of a treaty are primarily to be gathered from the text of the treaty and particularly from the preamble.[59] If the Convention rules are applied in this sense—that is to say, if consideration of the object and purpose is largely confined to the terms of the treaty itself—the danger that teleological interpretation will involve an excessive departure from the text is minimised; it is in any event clear that, within the framework of the Convention regime, consideration of the object and purpose is only one element of the general rule, and a subsidiary element at that.

To conclude on this topic of treaty interpretation, it should be noted that the Convention rules on interpretation draw a clear distinction between what de Visscher refers to as the 'intrinsic' and the 'extrinsic' techniques of interpretation.[60] The intrinsic method utilises only those elements which are contained in the

[56] *Op. cit.*, p. 255.
[57] 1966 I.L.C. Reports, p. 50.
[58] See Chaumont in 129 *Recueil des Cours* (1970), pp. 470–83.
[59] Jacobs, *loc. cit.*, p. 337.
[60] *Problèmes d'Interprétation Judiciaire en Droit International Public* (1963), pp. 50 *et seq.*

treaty itself and the extrinsic method utilises elements external to the treaty. Clearly, the text of the treaty itself is the principal intrinsic element, but so also is the *context of the treaty*, which the Convention defines as comprising any agreement relating to the treaty made between all the parties in connection with the conclusion of the treaty and any instrument made by one or more parties in connection with the conclusion of the treaty and accepted by the other parties as an instrument related to the treaty. It should be noted that this definition of the context is deliberately narrow, in the sense that it is confined to documents drawn up in connection with the conclusion of the treaty. Subsequent agreements or subsequent practice in the application of the treaty, together with any relevant rules of international law applicable in the relations between the parties are treated rather as extrinsic elements which have to be taken into account together with the context. The reference to 'relevant rules of international law applicable in the relations between the parties' may be taken to include not only the general rules of international law but also treaty obligations existing for the parties.[61]

IV TREATIES AND THIRD STATES

Articles 34–38 of the Convention, which deal with treaties and third States, do not call for extensive comment. The maxim *pacta tertiis nec nocent nec prosunt* is supported both by general legal principle and by common sense. In so far as a treaty may bear the attributes of a contract, third States are clearly strangers to that contract. Such problems as exist in international law about the relationship of third States to a treaty concern the scope of the exceptions to the general principle.

The rule laid down in Article 34 that a treaty does not create either obligations or rights for a third State without its consent is unexceptionable as a statement of principle. So far as obligations are concerned, it has been confirmed by the Permanent Court in the 'Free Zones' case[62] and in the 'River Oder' case;[63] as a matter of treaty law, the rule admits of no exceptions in the case of obligations, although this is, of course, without prejudice to the principle that

[61] *Official Records, Second Session,* 13th plenary meeting (Fleischauer).
[62] P.C.I.J. (1932), Series A/B, No. 46, p. 41.
[63] P.C.I.J. (1929), Series A, No. 23, pp. 19–22.

certain obligations stipulated in a treaty may bind third States independently as customary rules of international law. So far as rights are concerned, there are doctrinal differences between those jurists who claim that, at most, a treaty can confer a *benefit* on a third State, which can be transformed into a right only by some collateral agreement between the third State and the parties to the treaty,[64] and those jurists who maintain that there is nothing in international law to prevent two or more States from effectively creating a right in favour of another State by treaty if they so intend.[65] The two schools of thought differ as to the significance to be attached to the *dictum* of the Permanent Court in the 'Free Zones' case, where the Court stated:

> It cannot be lightly presumed that stipulations favourable to a third State have been adopted with the object of creating an actual right in its favour. There is however nothing to prevent the will of sovereign States from having this object and this effect. The question of the existence of a right acquired under an instrument drawn between other States is therefore one to be decided in each particular case: it must be ascertained whether the States which have stipulated in favour of a third State meant to create for that State an actual right which the latter has accepted as such.[66]

To McNair this is merely an *obiter dictum*, since the Court had expressly held that Switzerland had acquired true contractual rights by virtue of agreements made in the years 1815 and 1816 to which Switzerland was at that time a party and which had not been abrogated since. To those of the opposite persuasion, the *dictum* supports the view that the States parties to a treaty can confer true rights upon a third State, which the latter can invoke directly and on its own account.

Having regard to this doctrinal difference, it is probably best to regard Article 34 as merely establishing a presumption; certainly it must be read together with Articles 35–37, which set out the possible exceptions to the general principle, and Article 38, which preserves the principle that rules in a treaty may become binding on third States as customary principles of international law.

[64] See, for example, McNair, *op. cit.*, p. 312, and Rousseau, *Droit International Public* (1953), p. 53.

[65] For a summary of the conflicting viewpoints, see 1966 I.L.C. Reports, pp. 58–9.

[66] P.C.I.J. (1932), Series A/B, No. 46, pp. 147–8.

Article 35 provides that an obligation may arise for a third State from a provision of a treaty if two conditions are met:

(*a*) The parties to the treaty must have intended the provision to be the means of establishing the obligation; and
(*b*) The third State must have expressly accepted that obligation in writing.

It should be noted that this article is so worded as to make it clear that the juridical basis of the obligation for the third State is not the treaty itself but the collateral agreement whereby the third State has accepted the obligation. It should also be noted that the Convention contains, in Article 75, an express reservation about obligations which may arise for an aggressor State in consequence of measures taken in conformity with the Charter with reference to the aggression. The inclusion of Article 75 in the Convention results from certain governmental comments on the earlier draft articles proposed by the Commission to the effect that the rule stated in Article 35 should not apply with respect to treaty provisions imposed upon an aggressor State in consequence of action taken in conformity with the Charter.[67]

Article 36 deals with the converse case of rights arising for a third State from a provision of a treaty. For such a right to arise, two conditions must be satisfied:

(*a*) The parties to the treaty must have intended the provision to accord that right either to the third State, or to a group of States to which it belongs, or to all States; and
(*b*) The third State must have assented thereto, assent being presumed so long as the contrary is not indicated, unless the treaty has provided otherwise.

Article 36 also provides that a State exercising such a right must comply with the conditions for its exercise provided for in the treaty or established in conformity with the treaty. Of course, the right itself may be a conditional right. Thus Article 35(2) of the Charter of the United Nations stipulates that a State which is not a member of the United Nations may bring to the attention of the Security Council or of the General Assembly any dispute to which it is a party 'if it accepts in advance, for the purposes of the dispute, the obligations of pacific settlement provided in the present Charter'.

[67] See Kearney and Dalton, *loc. cit.*, p. 523.

In this case, the right itself is made subject to the fulfilment by the third State of the condition stipulated.[68]

The revocation or modification of obligations or rights arising for third States from the provisions of a treaty is covered by Article 37. Again, a distinction is drawn between obligations and rights. As regards obligations, the rule is stated to be that the obligation may be revoked or modified only with the consent of the parties to the treaty and the third State. Fortunately, this is expressed as a residuary rule. Theoretically, it is no doubt correct, since the obligation has arisen for the third State by virtue of a collateral agreement with the parties to the treaty, and it is this collateral agreement which must be revoked or modified. But, in practice, the rule may be rather artificial, since circumstances can be envisaged in which the parties to the treaty would simply wish to release the third State from further performance of the obligation.

As regards the revocation or modification of rights, the rule is expressed that a right which has arisen for a third State may not be revoked or modified by the parties if it is established that the right was intended not to be revocable or subject to modification without the consent of the third State. There are conflicting considerations here. On the one hand, States would no doubt be reluctant to stipulate rights in favour of third States if the effect of so doing would be to limit their freedom of action to modify or terminate the treaty. On the other hand, it is important that rights stipulated in favour of third States, particularly if they relate to such matters as rights of passage through international waterways, should have a firm and solid basis. The rule now embodied in the Convention seeks to resolve these conflicting considerations and would appear to be generally satisfactory.

Finally, Article 38, which we have already considered, merely saves the principle that rules contained in a treaty may become binding upon third States as customary rules of international law recognised as such.

V AMENDMENT AND MODIFICATION OF TREATIES

Articles 39–41 concern the amendment and modification of treaties. This is an area where State practice diverges to some extent from

[68] Jimenez de Arechega, 'Treaty stipulations in favour of third States', 50 *A.J.I.L.* (1956), pp. 255–6.

what is often asserted to be the rule of customary international law, namely, that a treaty may not be revised without the consent of all the parties.[69]

The Commission, in proposing the series of provisions which now constitute Articles 39–41 drew a clear distinction between 'amendment' and 'modification'. Amendment was said to denote a *formal* amendment of a treaty intended to alter its provisions with respect to all the parties, while modification was used in connection with an *inter se* agreement concluded between certain of the parties only, and intended to vary provisions of the treaty between themselves alone.[70] Although, in theory, there may be something to be said for this distinction, the position is not quite so clear-cut in practice. For one thing, the parties to a treaty may set out with the intention of formally amending the treaty. But one or more of the parties may fail to ratify the amending instrument, in which case the eventual result may be an *inter se* modification; even if all the parties do ratify the amending instrument there will inevitably be a certain lapse of time before they do so, during which period the amending instrument, if it has entered into force, will presumably operate as an *inter se* modification. Then there is the converse case where two or more of the parties to a treaty deliberately set out with the intention of negotiating an *inter se* modification; but this *inter se* modification may be open to acceptance by other parties to the treaty and, if accepted, may eventually operate as a formal amendment.

Thus, it will be seen that the distinction between formal amendment and *inter se* modification is by no means as clear-cut as the Convention regime might suggest. No doubt it is possible to determine whether the *initial* intent of the parties was to engage in a process of formal amendment or in a process of *inter se* modification; but the end result may differ from the initial intent.

Article 39 lays down the general rule that a treaty may be amended by agreement between the parties. Clearly, in the case of a bilateral treaty, the agreement of both parties is required; but, in the case of a multilateral treaty, agreement among *all* the parties is

[69] Hoyt, *The Unanimity Rule in the Revision of Treaties* (1959), contains a useful survey of State practice. See also Blix, 'The rule of unanimity in the revision of treaties', 5 *I.C.L.Q.* (1956), pp. 447–65 and 581–96, for a study of the procedures adopted for the revision of the treaties governing the international status of Tangier.

[70] 1966 I.L.C. Reports, p. 62.

not required, having regard to the modern practice of amending multilateral treaties by another multilateral treaty which comes into force only for those States which become bound by it.[71] Article 39 then goes on to lay down that the rules contained in Part II of the Convention concerning the conclusion and entry into force of treaties apply to an amending agreement except in so far as the treaty may otherwise provide. As the Convention applies only to treaties in written form, the question was raised at the conference whether an oral agreement to amend a treaty was permissible. The Expert Consultant, Sir Humphrey Waldock, pointed out that the Commission 'had recognised that in some cases treaties, especially those in simplified form, were varied by informal procedures and even by oral agreement of Ministers'; in his view, amendment by oral agreement would be covered by the general reservation about international agreements not in written form which was contained in Article 3.[72]

Article 40 contains complex residuary rules about the amendment of multilateral treaties. Its effect may be summarised as follows:

(*a*) A proposal to amend a multilateral treaty must be notified to all the contracting States, each of which becomes entitled to participate in the negotiation and conclusion of any amending agreement.

(*b*) A State entitled to become a party to a treaty also has the right to become a party to the treaty as amended.

(*c*) The amending agreement does not bind any State party to the original treaty which does not become a party to the amending agreement.

(*d*) A State which becomes a party to a treaty after it has been amended is, failing the expression of a contrary intention, considered to be a party to the treaty as amended, and a party to the unamended treaty in relation to any party to the treaty not bound by the amending agreement.

These rules prompt several comments. The first is that while it is no doubt right in principle to stipulate that any proposal to amend a multilateral treaty must be notified to all the parties, it is often very difficult for a depositary government or institution to comply with this requirement. This may be because one or more of the original parties have lost their identity and there is doubt as to

[71] *Ibid.* [72] *Official Records, First Session,* 37th meeting.

whether successor States have inherited rights and obligations under the original treaty. It may equally result from the consideration that the parties to the original treaty may be divided in their views as to whether certain territorial entities are to be considered as States. Thus the rule as stated in the Convention could, in theory, constitute an obstacle to the revision of treaties; but State practice reveals that there may be ways of circumventing this difficulty—for example, by the conclusion of a new treaty as opposed to the revision of an existing treaty. In such a case, of course, the rules set out in Article 30 would apply in the event that one or more of the parties to the later treaty failed to give notice of termination of the earlier treaty in accordance with the terms of the latter.

It should be noted that the International Labour Organisation has particular rules governing the procedure for the revision of Conventions and the legal consequences of revision. In the majority of cases *inter se* modification is excluded as being incompatible with the effective execution of the object and purpose of the treaty as a whole; but a few international labour Conventions expressly permit the modification of certain provisions by *inter se* agreement, on condition that the rights of other parties are not affected and that the *inter se* agreement affords equivalent protection.[73] These special rules are, of course, preserved by virtue of Article 5 of the Vienna Convention.

Article 41 sets out the circumstances in which two or more of the parties to a multilateral treaty may agree to modify the treaty as between themselves. The first, and most obvious case, is where the original treaty specifically provides for the possibility of an *inter se* modification; here it is quite clear that the parties intended to admit the possibility of 'contracting out'. But what is the position where the original treaty does not admit of this possibility? State practice furnishes many instances of *inter se* modication having been effected even where the original treaty did not admit of 'contracting out'; but, as the Commission rightly point out, 'an *inter se* agreement is more likely [than an amendment] to have an aim and effect incompatible with the object and purpose of the treaty'.[74] Accordingly, Article 41 imposes three conditions on the conclusion of *inter se* agreements, where such agreements are not contemplated in the original treaty:

[73] See statement by Mr Jenks in *Official Records, First Session,* 7th meeting.
[74] 1966 I.L.C. Reports, p. 65.

(*a*) The modification in question must not be prohibited by the treaty.

(*b*) It must not affect the enjoyment by the other parties of their rights under the treaty or the performance of their obligations; and

(*c*) It must not relate to a provision derogation from which would be incompatible with the effective execution of the object and purpose of the treaty as a whole.

The first of these conditions is self-evident and unexceptionable. The second and third conditions may prove to be unduly onerous in practice for would-be 'modifying' States, particularly where it is a question of seeking to modify a technical Convention in the field of international communications which is essentially of a regulatory character. A change in international regulations of this nature (for example, in relation to rules for the safety of life at sea) must of practical necessity take effect *erga omnes*, and will therefore fall foul of the rule prohibiting *inter se* modification in cases where the enjoyment by the other parties of their rights under the treaty is affected. In practice, it may be that would-be 'modifying' States will seek to overcome this difficulty by the simple device of concluding a completely new Convention.

CHAPTER IV

THE INVALIDITY, TERMINATION AND SUSPENSION OF OPERATION OF TREATIES

I intend to devote this chapter to the series of articles in the Vienna Convention which relate to the invalidity, termination and suspension of operation of treaties. But I shall deal separately, in the concluding chapter, with the concept that conflict with a peremptory norm of general international law (that is to say, a norm of *jus cogens*) may render a treaty void; I will also discuss, in my last lecture, the Convention provisions for the settlement of disputes arising out of the entire series of articles concerning the invalidity, termination and suspension of operation of treaties. I have made this distinction largely for reasons of convenience. The principle that conflict with a norm of *jus cogens* may render a treaty void is highly controversial and accordingly requires rather fuller analysis than would be possible if it were treated on a par with the other grounds of invalidity set out in the Convention. At the same time, there is a link between the Convention provisions on *jus cogens* and those on the settlement of disputes in the sense that special arrangements are made for the resolution of disputes concerning the interpretation or application of the Convention provisions on *jus cogens*.

I TERMINOLOGY IN PART V OF THE VIENNA CONVENTION

Part V of the Vienna Convention consists of some thirty articles. It consists of five sections under the headings 'General provisions' (Articles 42–45), 'Invalidity of treaties' (Articles 46–53), 'Termination and suspension of operation of treaties' (Articles 54–64), 'Procedure' (Articles 65–68) and 'Consequences of the invalidity, termination and suspension of the operation of a treaty' (Articles 69–72). Before proceeding to discuss these various sections, it is necessary to say a word about the terminology utilised in Part V, since, regrettably, the drafting of many of the articles is somewhat obscure. The difficulty arises primarily because of the use of the expression 'the invalidity of a treaty' to cover both those cases where, by virtue of the Convention, a treaty is rendered void *ab initio* and those cases were a State is entitled to invoke a particular ground as invalidating its consent to be bound by the treaty. It will be noted that Articles 46–50 inclusive of the Convention set out, in negative or positive form, a series of grounds which a State may invoke as invalidating its consent to be bound by a treaty. Article 51 deals with the special case where the expression of a State's consent to be bound by a treaty has been procured by the coercion of its representative and provides that the expression of consent is without any legal effect. Finally, Articles 52 and 53 are concerned with those cases in which the treaty itself is void by reason of considerations of what one might term international public policy (coercion of a State by the threat or use of force and conflict with a norm of *jus cogens*).

Part of the terminological difficulty stems from the fact that the Convention makes no clear distinction between bilateral and multilateral treaties. In the case of a bilateral treaty the distinction between absolute nullity and voidability is material only so far as the *consequences* are concerned; the legal effect of establishing a ground whereby the consent of one party to a bilateral treaty is invalidated is precisely the same as the legal effect of absolute nullity —the treaty falls to the ground. But in the case of a multilateral treaty different considerations apply. Absolute nullity means that the treaty has no legal force; but the establishment of a ground whereby the consent of a particular State to a multilateral treaty is invalidated will not cause the treaty as a whole to fall to the ground—the treaty will continue to be valid as between the remaining parties, and only the relations between that particular State and the parties to the treaty will be affected.[1]

The point is one of some importance, since reference is made in some provisions of the Convention (notably Articles 44 and 45) to the expression 'a ground for invalidating . . . a treaty'. It is quite clear from the context in which this expression is used that it is intended to cover, in addition to those cases in which the treaty as a whole becomes invalid, those cases where it is simply the consent of one State to a multilateral treaty which becomes invalidated.

[1] Article 69(4) of the Convention recognises the distinction by making special reference to the consequences which flow from the 'invalidity' of a particular State's consent to a multilateral treaty.

II GENERAL INTRODUCTION TO PART V

Part V of the Convention provoked lengthy and serious debates at both sessions of the Vienna conference. The reason is not far to seek. The spelling out in conventional form of a long series of separate and unrelated grounds for the avoidance of treaties is a disturbing phenomenon for the vast majority of international lawyers, who see in the principle *pacta sunt servanda* the principal safeguard for the security of treaties and other international transactions. Prior to the conclusion of the Vienna Convention most writers and publicists on the law of treaties had concentrated attention on the conditions for the essential validity of treaties. Thus McNair devotes a chapter of his magisterial work to 'Essential validity', discussing under this rubric the vitiating effect of coercion, mistake and incompatibility or conflict with rules of international law or treaty obligations.[2] Fitzmaurice and Waldock, as Special Rapporteurs on the law of treaties, also approached this topic from the standpoint of setting out the principles governing the essential validity of treaties,[3] Fitzmaurice cautiously prefacing his report on the matter by pointing to the paucity of material on essential validity, and the potentially misleading nature of private law analogies.

The Commission, however, preferred to group the conditions of essential validity under the general heading 'Invalidity of treaties', thus creating the unfortunate impression (even if the impression is misleading) that there existed no real presumption in favour of the validity of treaties. There is something to be said for the view advanced by Nahlik that a *positive* approach to the drafting of Part V of the Convention might have been preferable to the *negative* approach favoured by the Commission and endorsed by the conference.[4] But what is perhaps even more significant is that the drafting method adopted by the Commission required an exhaustive catalogue of all possible grounds of invalidity, no matter how theoretical and how little supported by State practice and international jurisprudence. This tends to reinforce the disturbing psychological impact of according authoritative expression to so

[2] *Op. cit.*, pp. 206–36.

[3] See Fitzmaurice, 'Third Report on the Law of Treaties', A/CN.4/115 of 18 March 1958, and Waldock, 'Second Report on the Law of Treaties,' A/CN.4/156 of 20 March 1963.

[4] *Loc. cit.*, pp. 738–9.

many apparent exceptions to the principle *pacta sunt servanda*. These considerations explain in part the anxiety evinced by many delegations, particularly from Western Europe and Latin America, about the content of Part V of the Convention, and their insistence that the inclusion of controversial grounds of invalidity must be accompanied by automatically available third-party procedures for the settlement of disputes arising on the interpretation or application of the series of articles in this Part of the Convention.

Article 42 of the Convention lays down that the validity of a treaty or of the consent of a State to be bound by a treaty may be impeached only through the application of the present Convention. The Commission had explained in their commentary that the phrase 'application of the present articles' (the last word was changed to 'Convention' at the conference) referred not merely to the particular article dealing with the particular ground of invalidity or termination but also to other articles governing the conditions for putting that article into effect, notably the articles dealing with procedure (now Articles 65–68).[5] This is a most important explanation of the underlying meaning of Article 42, since it confirms that the procedural safeguards set out in Articles 65–68 are applicable whenever a State party to the Convention seeks to invoke, as against another State party, one of the grounds of invalidity set out in Articles 46–53.

The wording of Article 42 also makes it clear that the grounds of invalidity, termination, denunciation, withdrawal or suspension of the operation of a treaty, as set out in the later articles in Part V, are exhaustive of all such grounds, leaving aside the operation of rules relating to State succession, State responsibility and the outbreak of hostilities on treaties which are excepted from the scope of the Convention by virtue of Article 73. Attention has already been drawn to the fact that the exhaustive nature of the catalogue of grounds of invalidity in Part V has led to the inclusion of several provisions whose foundation in positive international law is, to say the least, dubious and uncertain.

III ACQUIESCENCE

Article 45 embodies one of the essential safeguards operating to protect the stability of treaty relations—namely, the principle of

[5] 1966 I.L.C. Reports, p. 66.

acquiescence. This principle derives support from two cases decided by the International Court of Justice, the 'Arbitral award made by the King of Spain' case[6] and the 'Temple' case.[7] The effect of Article 45 is to prohibit a State from claiming that a treaty is invalid on grounds of lack of competence, restrictions on authority to express consent, error, fraud or corruption, or from seeking to terminate or suspend the operation of a treaty on grounds of material breach or fundamental change of circumstances if, after becoming aware of the facts, the State has expressly agreed that the treaty is valid or must, by reason of its conduct, be considered as having acquiesced in the validity of the treaty or its maintenance in force or in operation. It should be noted that there are differences between the principle of acquiescence and the operation of estoppel, although the effect may, in particular circumstances, be very similar. But where acquiescence is an element in the establishment of title to territory by prescription, what must be proved is the acquiescence of States generally, or at least those States adversely affected by the claim. By way of contrast, estoppel is a matter of adjectival, rather than substantive, law and accordingly the effect of a true estoppel is confined to the parties.[8] It is also relevant that estoppel is a concept of general application, the essential aim of which is to preclude a party from benefiting by his own inconsistency to the detriment of another party who has in good faith relied upon a representation of fact made by the former party.

For these reasons, it would be wrong to regard Article 45 as imposing restrictions upon the circumstances in which an estoppel may be invoked before an international tribunal in relation to a treaty dispute. The operation of estoppel is presumably admissible, under customary international law, in relation to the application of all articles of the Convention except those laying down grounds of absolute nullity, e.g. coercion or conflict with an existing norm of *jus cogens*.

One final point may be noted here. At the conference an amendment to delete what is now sub-paragraph (b) of Article 45 was

[6] *I.C.J. Reports* (1960), pp. 213–14.

[7] *I.C.J. Reports* (1962), pp. 23–32. Note also the discussion of the principles in the Argentina–Chile Palena arbitration; *Award of Her Majesty Queen Elizabeth II* (1966), p. 66; 38 *International Law Reports*, p. 10.

[8] Bowett, *Estoppel before International Tribunals and its relation to Acquiescence*, 33 *B.Y.I.L.* (1957), pp. 176–202.

proposed by the delegations of Bolivia, Byelorussia, Colombia, the Dominican Republic, Guatemala, the U.S.S.R., Venezuela and the Congo (Brazzaville). This amendment was defeated by a substantial majority, but it is a matter for ironical comment that a substantial proportion of this rather disparate group of co-sponsoring States are currently involved in territorial disputes raising, sometimes in an acute form, questions concerning the application of the principle of acquiescence.

IV SPECIFIC GROUNDS FOR INVALIDATING CONSENT TO BE BOUND

The Convention lays down four specific grounds which may be invoked as invalidating the consent of a State to be bound by a treaty. These are:

(*a*) Violation of certain provisions of internal law regarding competence to conclude treaties.
(*b*) Error.
(*c*) Fraud.
(*d*) Corruption of a representative of State.

I will discuss briefly each of these grounds.

I VIOLATION OF INTERNAL LAW

The question whether the violation of a provision of internal law regarding competence to conclude treaties constitutes a ground which the State concerned may invoke as invalidating its consent to be bound is an issue which has long divided international lawyers. In the main, doctrine is divided between what may, for purposes of convenience, be termed the constitutionalist and the internationalist schools.[9] The constitutionalist school holds that international law leaves it to internal law to determine the organs and procedures by which the consent of a State to be bound by a treaty is formed and expressed, and that violation of a prescription of internal law renders void (or voidable) the expression of a State's consent to be bound. The internationalist school bases itself upon the theory that international law is concerned only with the external manifestations of the expression of a State's consent to be bound, and that the act of an agent who is competent under international law to bind the

[9] Hostert, *loc cit.*, pp. 100–9.

State and apparently authorised to do so in the particular case binds the State even if a prescription of internal law has not been complied with.[10] Between the two extremes there are those who, while adhering in principle to the constitutionalist school, attempt to soften its impact by laying down that only those constitutional limitations which are 'notorious' need be taken into account by other States, so that a State contesting the validity of a treaty on the grounds of a violation of internal law may invoke only those provisions of its constitution which are notorious.

Within the Commission, there was a gradual shift of opinion on this issue over the years. The first two Special Rapporteurs (Messrs Brierly and Lauterpacht) put forward drafts based upon the constitutionalist position, in the belief that governments would reject any other rule. Fitzmaurice, however, broke with tradition, advancing unequivocally the proposition that 'consent means consent on the international plane, and the reality of such consent is not impaired by the fact that, on the domestic plane, certain consents are lacking; or that there has otherwise been a failure by the State concerned, or its authorities, to observe the correct constitutional processes . . . for the purpose of proceeding to signature; or to keep within any limitations on the treaty-making power imposed by the domestic law or constitution'.[11] Waldock also favoured the internationalist theory, although with some qualifications.[12] Majority opinion within the Commission eventually coalesced on the principle that non-observance of a provision of internal law regarding competence to enter into treaties does not affect the validity of a consent given in due form by a State organ or agent competent under international law to give that consent. But the majority were persuaded to admit an exception in the case where the violation of a provision of internal law regarding competence to conclude treaties was absolutely manifest.

At the conference an amendment tabled by Pakistan and Japan proposed to delete the 'manifest violation' exception. This was defeated by a fairly substantial majority. On the other hand, it was apparent that the conference was rather uneasy about the danger to the security of treaties represented by the 'manifest violation'

[10] For a full survey of the conflicting theories, see Holloway, *Modern Trends in Treaty Law* (1967), pp. 123–33.

[11] A/CN.4/115, Article 10.

[12] A/CN.4/156, Article 5.

exception. For this reason, two significant proposals designed to narrow the scope of the exception and to define it more closely were adopted. The first proposal, tabled by Peru, required the violation not only to be manifest but also to relate to a rule of internal law 'of fundamental importance'. The second proposal, tabled by the United Kingdom, picked up a phrase from the Commission's commentary by requiring that a 'manifest violation' should be objectively evident to any State dealing with the matter normally and in good faith. With minor drafting variations, these two proposals were incorporated in the final text of Article 46.

Article 47 deals with the possibility of invoking, as a ground of invalidity, the failure of a representative to observe restrictions on his authority to express the consent of the State to be bound. Failure to observe such a restriction cannot be invoked as a ground of invalidity unless the restriction was notified to the other negotiating States prior to the expression of consent.

Having regard to the cumulative conditions set out in these two articles and to the negative manner in which they are drafted, it may be conceded that practical cases in which they could be invoked will be rather rare.[13]

2 ERROR

In customary international law, instances in which errors of substance have been invoked as a ground for vitiating consent are extremely rare. As the Commission point out, most of them concern errors in maps. The effect of error was considered by the Permanent Court of International Justice in the 'Eastern Greenland'[14] case and by the present International Court in the 'Temple' case.[15] In neither was the plea of error accepted, and the *dicta* in the two cases accordingly throw light primarily on the conditions under which error will *not* vitiate consent rather than on those under which it will do so.

Having regard to the paucity of material on error as a ground which may be invoked as invalidating consent, it is perhaps as well that the text proposed by the Commission, and in substance accepted by the conference as Article 48, is drafted in suitably restrictive

[13] Nahlik, *loc. cit.*, p. 741.

[14] P.C.I.J., Series A/B, No. 53, pp. 71 and 91.

[15] *I.C.J. Reports* (1962), p. 26.

terms. Error may be invoked as a ground for invalidating consent only if:

(*a*) the error relates to a fact or situation which was assumed by the State invoking the error to exist at the time when the treaty was concluded; and
(*b*) that fact or situation formed an essential basis of its consent to be bound by the treaty.

Furthermore, error may not be invoked by a State if it contributed by its own conduct to the error or if the circumstances were such as to put the State on notice of a possible error.

Although the text of Article 48 uses the expression 'error *in* a treaty', it should be noted that this is intended to mean any error of fact *relating* to a treaty.[16] Thus an error in the calculation of the capacity of turbines underlying a treaty for the sharing of hydro-electric power would presumably constitute an error capable of being invoked under this article.[17]

Earlier Special Rapporteurs, notably Fitzmaurice, had sought to distinguish between unilateral error and mutual error, maintaining that unilateral error could be invoked only if the error had been induced by the fraud, fraudulent misrepresentation, concealment or non-disclosure, or culpable negligence, of the other party. The Commission, however, took the view that international law did not distinguish between mutual error and unilateral error, the distinction being relevant only in certain legal systems.

Finally, it was made clear at the conference that cases of innocent misrepresentation (as opposed to fraudulent representation) would not affect the validity of consent unless the innocent misrepresentation led to an error which could be invoked as invalidating consent. In certain circumstances, innocent misrepresentation by one party might help to defeat the suggestion that the other party ought to have discovered the error.[18]

[16] See explanation given by Sir Humphrey Waldock: *Official Records, First Session*, 45th meeting.

[17] This was an example given by the United States delegation; see *Official Records, First Session*, 44th meeting (Kearney).

[18] Explanation given by Sir Humphrey Waldock in response to a question posed by the representative of Ceylon (Pinto) at the 44th meeting of the Committee of the Whole: *Official Records, First Session*, 45th meeting.

3 FRAUD

Examples of fraud as a ground for vitiating consent to be bound by a treaty are rare, if not non-existent, in State practice. The Commission, in their commentary to what is now Article 49, were unable to cite a single instance of fraud, admitting that 'the paucity of precedents means that there is little guidance to be found either in practice or in the jurisprudence of international tribunals as to the scope to be given to the concept'.[19] Writers and publicists have of course long accepted the principle that fraud exercised by a negotiating State to induce the conclusion of a treaty with another State may entitle the latter to claim that its consent to the treaty has been vitiated. Thus McNair draws attention to the general agreement among writers that 'a treaty concluded as the result of a fundamental mistake induced in one party . . . by the fraud of another party is void, or at least voidable'.[20] Guggenheim treats fraud as being one of the 'vices de volonté',[21] while Rousseau mentions fraud as being a ground of invalidity, while admitting the lack of concrete international practice in the matter.[22]

At the conference the delegations of Chile and Malaysia tabled a proposal to delete the Commission's draft article on fraud. It was argued that the Commission's text was based on 'the mechanical and unconsidered application of rules of internal private law to public international law' and that the complex procedure for the conclusion of treaties, involving the participation of capable and experienced officials, rendered it extremely unlikely that governments would be unable to take the necessary precautions to protect their interests.[23] Other delegations sought to invoke examples of fraud in State practice, the Soviet delegation citing the example of a treaty concluded between Italy and Ethiopia in 1899. Interestingly, the Ethiopian delegation (which nonetheless supported the retention of the article on fraud) denied that this was a case of fraud, pointing out that the dispute had arisen because of a discrepancy between the Italian and Amharic texts of the treaty; it was

[19] 1966 I.L.C. Reports, p. 73.
[20] *Op. cit.*, p. 211.
[21] *Traité de Droit international Public*, vol. 1 (1953), p. 92.
[22] *Principes Généraux de Droit International Public*, vol. 1, p. 351.
[23] *Official Records, First Session*, 45th meeting (Vargas).

thus a case of error striking at the roots of the treaty.[24] Notwithstanding the absence of State practice on fraud as a ground for vitiating consent to be bound by a treaty, the conference rejected the Chilean and Malaysian proposal. It also rejected an amendment tabled by the United States delegation and designed to incorporate two additional limitations in the text—that there should have been 'reasonable reliance' upon the fraudulent conduct and that the conduct should have concerned a fact or situation 'of material importance' to the consent of the State concerned to be bound by the treaty.[25]

4 CORRUPTION OF A REPRESENTATIVE OF A STATE

If instances of fraud are rare enough in State practice, examples of corruption being invoked as a ground for invalidating consent to be bound by a treaty are non-existent. The Commission's commentary is strikingly devoid of any incident in which it has been alleged that the consent of a State to be bound by a treaty has been procured by the corruption of its representative. It was only at the final session of the Commission in 1966 that a specific provision establishing corruption as a separate ground of invalidity was written into the set of draft articles presented by the Commission. The commentary discloses that the members of the Commission were divided in their views as to whether corruption should be regarded as a separate ground of invalidity. Some maintained that corruption was not an independent cause of defective consent, but merely one of the possible means of securing consent through fraudulent conduct; but the majority were of the view 'that the corruption of a representative by another negotiating State undermines the consent which the representative purports to express on behalf of his State in a quite special manner which differentiates the case from one of fraud'.[26]

Again, an attempt was made at the conference by the delegation of Chile, Japan and Mexico to secure the deletion of this provision, the sponsors maintaining that corruption was simply another form of fraud and that the vagueness of the wording might lead to

[24] *Loc. cit.*, 47th meeting (Kebreth).

[25] A/Conf. 39/C.1/L.276. See Kearney and Dalton, *loc cit.*, p. 528.

[26] 1966 I.L.C. Reports, p. 74.

abuses; but the proposal to delete Article 50 from the text of the Convention was defeated by a fairly substantial majority.

The Commission, in their commentary, seek to limit the scope of the provision by indicating that the expression 'corruption' is used 'expressly in order to indicate that only acts calculated to exercise a substantial influence on the disposition of the representative to conclude the treaty' may be invoked and that 'a small courtesy or favour' shown to a representative cannot be invoked as a pretext for invalidating a treaty.[27] This explanation does little to clarify the meaning of the text. The distinction between a substantial inducement and a small courtesy or favour is self-evidently a matter for subjective appreciation. It is to be feared that the inclusion of corruption as a separate ground of invalidity will make it easier for a State to repudiate a representative who may have exceeded his instructions. There is no doubt a practical safeguard in that States will be reluctant to admit that their own representatives have been corrupted; but, of course, a revolutionary regime wishing to escape from an inconvenient treaty concluded by a previous government would be under no such inhibitions, since the corruption would be attributed to a representative of the ousted regime.

V COERCION

Articles 51 and 52 deal with two separate aspects of coercion—coercion of a representative of a State in order to procure the conclusion of a treaty and coercion of the State itself by the threat or use of force.

I will discuss first the question of coercion of a representative of a State. Article 51 provides that the expression of a State's consent to be bound by a treaty which has been procured by the coercion of its representative through acts or threats directed against him shall be without any legal effect. There is no doubt that duress exercised against the person of a representative concluding a treaty has long been recognised by jurists as an element which may vitiate the consent of the State to be bound by the treaty,[28] although it has been suggested that if the treaty requires ratification and has been knowingly ratified the State may no longer invoke duress

[27] *Ibid.*

[28] McNair, *op. cit.*, p. 207; O'Connell, *op. cit.*, p. 239.

exercised against its representative to procure signature.[29] The draft article proposed by the Commission did not include this qualification.

At the conference the text of what is now Article 51 was criticised on the grounds that, as drafted:

(*a*) It might be thought to enable the coercing State to claim that the treaty was null and void.

(*b*) It did not specifically exclude the possibility that a third State might seek to claim that a treaty between two other States was rendered null and void by reason of coercion directed against a representative.

(*c*) It did not give the injured State the option to retain the treaty if it decided that, on balance and despite the vice of coercion, the benefits of maintaining the treaty in force outweighed the loss which would occur if the treaty were terminated.[30]

It is doubtful whether there is much substance in point (*a*). One would assume in any event that the operation of general principles of law (*ex turpi causa non oritur jus*) would preclude the making of any claim by the coercing State. Points (*b*) and (*c*) are of more significance, and no effective answer was vouchsafed to them at the conference. Nevertheless, it is perhaps not very likely that a third State would seek to deny the validity of a treaty concluded between two other States on this ground; and the wording of Article 51 indicates that it will apply almost exclusively to duress exercised against a representative to procure signature, since it is difficult to envisage circumstances in which duress could be exercised against an *individual* (as distinct from the State) to procure ratification.

Article 52 gave rise to lengthy discussions at the conference. The concept that a treaty may be void if its conclusion has been procured by the threat or use of force is of very recent origin. The traditional doctrine was that a treaty is not rendered null and void, or voidable at the instance of one of the parties, by reason only of the fact that such party was coerced by the other party into concluding it, whether the coercion is applied at the time of signature or of ratification or at both times.[31] It was accepted that

[29] Harvard Research, Article 32(a); 29 *A.J.I.L. Supplement* (1935), pp. 1148–59.

[30] *Official Records, First Session*, 47th Meeting (Briggs).

[31] McNair, *op. cit.*, p. 208; Fauchille, *Traité de Droit International Public*, vol. 1, Part 3 (1926), p. 298; de Louter, *Le Droit International Public Positif*, vol. 1 (1920), p. 478; Hall, *op. cit.*, p. 381; de Visscher, *Théories et Réalités en Droit International Public* (1960), pp. 313–14.

treaties procured by the threat or use of force were morally questionable, but it was argued that to place the stigma of invalidity upon treaties procured by the threat or use of force would place in jeopardy all peace treaties entered into on the conclusion of hostilities.

The traditional doctrine became established at the time when force as an instrument of national policy was not outlawed. With the gradual development of the principle prohibiting the threat or use of force in international relations, now embodied in Article 2(4) of the United Nations Charter, the foundations of the traditional doctrine were shaken. As the Commission put it in their commentary to what is now Article 52:

> With the Covenant [of the League of Nations] and the Pact of Paris there began to develop a strong body of opinion which held that treaties [brought about by the threat or use of force] should no longer be recognised as legally valid. The endorsement of the criminality of aggressive war in the Charters of the Allied Military Tribunals for the trial of the Axis war criminals, the clear-cut prohibition of the threat or use of force in Article 2(4) of the Charter of the United Nations, together with the practice of the United Nations itself, have reinforced and consolidated this development in the law. The Commission considers that these developments justify the conclusion that the invalidity of a treaty procured by the illegal threat or use of force is a principle which is *lex lata* in the international law of today.[32]

Two distinct issues were discussed at the conference in connection with the drafting of this Article. The first arose out of an amendment tabled by a group of nineteen Afro-Asian and Latin American countries which sought to define the expression 'force' as including any 'economic or political pressure'. As the text proposed by the Commission referred to 'the threat or use of force in violation of the principles of the Charter of the United Nations' it was clear that the nineteen-power amendment sought to put a gloss upon the wording of the Charter, and particularly of Article 2(4). The vast majority of the Western States represented at the conference, together with certain Latin American States, vigorously opposed the nineteen-power amendment, arguing that (*a*) the drafting history and text of the Charter clearly demonstrated that the expression 'force' as used in Article 2(4) referred only to physical or armed force, and (*b*) the acceptance of economic or political pressure as

[32] 1966 I.L.C. Reports, p. 75.

a sufficient ground for rendering a treaty null and void would seriously prejudice the stability of treaty relations, given the vagueness of the language employed and the varying interpretations which would undoubtedly be given to the concept of 'pressure'. That the sponsors of the nineteen-power amendment intended to give the broadest possible interpretation to the concept of 'pressure' emerged from the statements made in support of the amendment. The representative of Tanzania indicated that among the means of economic pressure which would render a treaty null and void would be 'the withdrawal of aid or of promises of aid, the recall of economic experts and so on'.[33] The representative of the United Arab Republic referred to economic pressure directed against developing countries, particularly those whose 'economy depended on a single crop or the export of a single product'.[34] The representative of Algeria claimed that economic pressure was 'a characteristic of neo-colonialism' and openly spelt out what would be the consequences of admitting that economic pressure could render a treaty null and void:

> Political independence could not be an end in itself; it was even illusory if it was not backed by genuine economic independence. That was why some countries had chosen the political, economic and social system they regarded as best calculated to overcome under-development as quickly as possible. That choice provoked intense opposition from certain interests which saw their privileges threatened and then sought through economic pressure to abolish or at least restrict the right of peoples of self-determination. Such neo-colonialist practices which affected more than two-thirds of the world's population and were retarding or nullifying all efforts to overcome under-development, should therefore be denounced with the utmost rigour.[35]

It is not unnatural that those delegations concerned to preserve the security and stability of treaties should regard such sweeping statements with intense misgivings. Acceptance of the concept that economic pressure could operate to render a treaty null and void would appear, if these sweeping views as to the dominant position of developed countries were accepted, to invite claims which would put at risk any treaty concluded between a developing and a developed country.

[33] *Official Records, First Session*, 48th meeting (Bishota).
[34] *Ibid.*, 49th meeting (El Dessoui).
[35] *Ibid.*, 49th meeting (Haddad).

In the event, and after a major confrontation, the nineteen-power amendment was not pressed to a vote, since many Western delegations had hinted that its acceptance by the conference would seriously prejudice the prospect of producing a Convention which would command their support. Instead, a declaration condemning the threat or use of pressure in any form by a State to coerce any other State to conclude a treaty was adopted unanimously by the Committee of the Whole and eventually by the Plenary.

It should be noted that, during the debate on this issue, reference was made by many delegations to the parallel discussion being carried on within the framework of the Special Committee on Principles of International Law concerning Friendly Relations and Co-operation among States, where, in the context of the elaboration of the principle prohibiting the threat or use of force in international relations, a corresponding dispute had arisen as to the meaning of the term 'force'. The Declaration on Friendly Relations, adopted by the General Assembly at its twenty-fifth session in 1970,[36] papers over the difference on this point by failing to give any definition of the expression 'force'; but it would appear from a close study of the records of the Special Committee that a restrictive interpretation is called for.[37] The drafting history of Article 52 of the Vienna Convention would likewise seem to support the conclusion that nullity attaches only to those treaties procured by the threat or use of physical or armed force; but, of course, any extended interpretation of the Charter provisions on this point might have as a consequence that an extended interpretation would be given to Article 52.

The second point discussed at the conference in relation to Article 52 concerns the application *ratione temporis* of the rule laid down. The attention of the Commission had been drawn to this point in several governmental comments. The Commission, in their commentary to what is now Article 52, stated that it would be illogical and unacceptable to formulate the rule as applicable only from the date of the conclusion of a Convention on the law of treaties, since the invalidity of a treaty procured by the illegal threat or use of

[36] General Assembly resolution 2615 (xxv) of 24 October 1970; Brownlie, *Basic Documents in International Law*, second edition (1972) p. 32.

[37] Rosenstock, 'The declaration of principles of international law concerning friendly relations: a survey', 65 *A.J.I.L.* (1971), pp. 724–5.

force was a principle which was *lex lata*. After referring to Article 2(4) of the Charter, the Commission went on to say:

> The present article, by its formulation, recognises by implication that the rule which it lays down is applicable at any rate to all treaties concluded since the entry into force of the Charter. On the other hand, the Commission did not think that it was part of its function, in codifying the modern law of treaties, to specify on what precise date in the past an existing general rule in another branch of international law came to be established as such. Accordingly, it did not feel that it should go beyond the temporal indication given by the reference in the article to 'the principles of the Charter of the United Nations'.[38]

This was not good enough for the conference. A group of fourteen countries, led by Czechoslovakia, tabled an amendment to the Commission to refer to 'the principles of *international law embodied in* the Charter of the United Nations'.[39] It was explained that the purpose of this amendment was 'to specify the time element for the effect of the prohibition of resort to the threat or use of force', but the sponsors appeared to acknowledge the force of the Commission's observation that it would not be right, in codifying the law of treaties, to specify a precise date.[40] Reference was made by other speakers to the significance of the Covenant of the League of Nations and the Pact of Paris in the establishment of the modern law prohibiting the threat or use of force. In the event, the fourteen-power amendment was adopted by a large majority.

It is difficult to assess the significance of this in the light of the economy of the Convention as a whole. Article 4 of the Convention, adopted at the second session, makes it clear that the Convention as such has no retroactive application; but this rule is expressed to be 'without prejudice to the application of any rules set forth in the present Convention to which treaties would be subject under international law independently of the Convention'. Thus, it would no doubt be possible to invoke the rule stated in Article 52 with respect to a treaty concluded since the establishment of the modern law prohibiting the threat or use of force, but to invoke it only as a rule of customary international law. The wording of Article 52 in any event leaves wholly unresolved the question of the precise point in time at which the modern law crystallised.

[38] 1966 I.L.C. Reports, p. 76.
[39] A/Conf.39/C.1/L. 289.
[40] *Official Records, First Session*, 48th meeting (Smejkal).

VI TERMINATION AND SUSPENSION OF OPERATION OF TREATIES

Under this head I propose to discuss three topics: denunciation of a treaty containing no provision for termination, termination or suspension of the operation of a treaty as a consquence of its breach, and *rebus sic stantibus*.

I DENUNCIATION OF A TREATY CONTAINING NO PROVISION FOR TERMINATION

It goes without saying that a treaty may be terminated, or a party may withdraw from it, in accordance with the provisions of the treaty or by consent of all the parties; this self-evident rule is incorported in Article 54 of the Convention.

Article 56 deals with the more controversial issue of whether it is possible for a State to denounce or withdraw from a treaty which contains no provision regarding its termination. In theory, and having regard to the significance of the principle *pacta sunt servanda*, the answer should be in the negative; but doctrine and State practice have long recognised the existence of certain strictly limited exceptions to the general rule. The Commission submitted, in their final set of draft articles, a text which admitted the possibility of unilateral denunciation or withdrawal only where 'it is established that the parties intended to admit the possibility of denunciation or withdrawal'. They explained that 'under this rule, the character of the treaty is only one of the elements to be taken into account, and a right of denunciation or withdrawal will not be implied unless it appears from the general circumstances of the case that the parties intended to allow the possibility of unilateral denunciation or withdrawal'.[41]

The very limited nature of this exception was challenged at the conference. Respectable authority was invoked for the proposition that a right of unilateral denunciation might be implied from the character or nature of the treaty alone. Thus Fitzmaurice, in his 'Second Report on the Law of Treaties', had drawn attention to the general conviction that 'there are certain sorts of treaties which, unless entered into for a fixed and stated period or expressed to

41 1966 I.L.C. Reports, p. 80.

be in perpetuity, are *by their nature* such that any of the parties to them have an implied right to bring them to an end or to withdrawal from them'.[42] As examples, Fitzmaurice cited treaties of alliance and commercial or trading agreements. In the same sense, Brierly had suggested that there were certain types of treaty which, from the nature of the subject matter or the circumstances in which they were concluded, might be presumed to be susceptible of denunciation even though they contain no express term to that effect. 'A *modus vivendi* is an obvious illustration; treaties of alliance and commerce are probably in the same case, though in practice such treaties ordinarily have a fixed period of duration.'[43]

Following this general line of thought, the delegations of Cuba and the United Kingdom submitted separate amendments at the first session of the conference designed to establish that the character or nature of the treaty might alone be such as to justify an implication that unilateral denunciation was permissible. In the event, the United Kingdom amendment was adopted, and the text of Article 56 of the Convention now embodies two exceptions to the general rule:

(*a*) Where it is established that the parties intended to admit the possibility of denunciation or withdrawal.
(*b*) Where a right of denunciation or withdrawal may be implied by the nature of the treaty.

Two additional points should be noted in connection with Article 56. In the first place, it is quite clear that this article lays down a ground for termination independently of the other grounds of termination, denunciation or withdrawal provided for in the other articles of the Convention and in particular in Articles 52 and 62.[44] In the second place, although the text of Article 65 makes no specific reference to denunciation as such, it is clear that any State wishing to invoke Article 56 must notify the other parties to the treaty of its claim. This is confirmed by a statement of the chairman of the Drafting Committee at the second session of the conference.[45]

[42] A/CN.4/107 of 15 March 1957, p. 72. As regards the possibility of unilateral denunciation of commercial treaties, see McNair, *op. cit.*, pp. 504–5.
[43] Brierly, *The Law of Nations*, sixth edition (1963), p. 331.
[44] *Official Records, First Session*, 59th meeting (Small and Waldock).
[45] *Official Records, Second Session*, 25th plenary meeting (Yasseen).

2 TERMINATION OR SUSPENSION OF THE OPERATION OF A TREATY AS A CONSEQUENCE OF ITS BREACH

That a right of unilateral denunciation or termination of a treaty on the grounds of prior material breach by another party exists is attested to by jurists and confirmed by State practice.[46] The problems in this area concern the modalities of application of the principle.

Article 60 of the Convention lays down a series of residuary rules which may be summarised as follows:

(*a*) A material breach of a bilateral treaty by one of the parties entitles the other to invoke the breach as a ground for terminating the treaty or suspending its operation in whole or in part.

(*b*) A material breach of a multilateral treaty by one of the parties entitles the other parties by unanimous agreement to suspend the operation of the treaty in whole or in part or to terminate it either in relations between themselves and the defaulting State or generally.

(*c*) A material breach of a multilateral treaty by one of the parties entitles a party specially affected by the breach to invoke it as a ground for suspending the operation of the treaty as a whole or in part in relations between itself and the defaulting State.

(*d*) A material breach of a multilateral treaty by one of the parties entitles any party other than the defaulting State to invoke the breach as a ground for suspending the operation of the treaty in whole or in part with respect to itself if the treaty is of such a character that a material breach of its provisions by one party radically changes the position of every party with respect to the performance of its obligations under the treaty.

This summary of the rules laid down in Article 60 provokes the following observations. The consequences of a material breach of a bilateral treaty are no doubt correctly expressed under (*a*) above; it is in any event satisfactory that the exercise of the right of termination or suspension is optional at the discretion of the injured party

[46] For a recent survey of doctrinal opinion on this point, see Bhek Pati Sinha, *Unilateral Denunciation of Treaty because of Prior Violations of Obligations by other Party* (1966), pp. 5–34.

and that any injured party seeking to invoke the breach as a ground for termination or suspension must comply with the procedural safeguards set out in Article 65–68.

On the other hand, the rules concerning the consequences of a breach of a multilateral treaty are less satisfactorily expressed. In particular, the procedural safeguards in Articles 65–68 do not apply in the case where the parties to the treaty, other than the party alleged to be in breach, unanimously agree to suspend the operation of the treaty or to terminate it either in relations between themselves and the defaulting State or generally (rule (*b*) above). The justification for this appears to be that the requirement of unanimous agreement provides adequate guarantees against arbitrary action.[47] It is questionable whether this is correct; circumstances can certainly be envisaged where the party alleged to be in breach may be in the right, and *not* the other parties acting unanimously.

The rule under (*d*) above is designed to deal with breaches of special types of treaties, such as disarmament treaties, where a breach by one party tends to undermine the whole treaty regime in a very special manner. In the case of disarmament treaties, it is necessary for an innocent party to be able to protect itself against the threat resulting from the arming of the defaulting State, and accordingly to be permitted to claim release from obligations owed not only to the defaulting State but also to the other parties.[48]

Paragraph 4 of Article 60 provides, in effect, that material breach by one of the parties to a treaty does not operate as a ground for termination or suspension where the breach concerns provisions relating to the protection of the human person contained in treaties of a humanitarian character, in particular provisions prohibiting any form of reprisals against persons protected by such treaties. This paragraph was added to the text at the second session of the conference on a proposal by Switzerland. It constitutes a part-recognition of the principle advocated by Fitzmaurice according to which the rule of unilateral denunciation in the event of breach is inapplicable in the case of law-making treaties which embody absolute or unconditional obligations and not reciprocal obligations:

> This is because all rules of this particular character are intended not so much for the benefit of the States, as directly for the benefit of the

---

[47] *Official Records, Second Session*, 21st plenary meeting (Rosenne).

[48] 1966 I.L.C. Reports, p. 83.

individuals concerned, as human beings and on humanitarian grounds. In the same way, a breach by one party of a convention on human rights, a convention providing for the safety of life at sea, labour conventions regarding hours and conditions of work, etc. would not justify corresponding breaches of the treaty by other parties even *vis-à-vis* the treaty-breaking State and its nationals, for reasons of a broadly similar character. Such conventions involve obligations of an absolute and, so to speak, self-existent kind, the duty to perform which, once assumed, is not (as for instance with commercial treaties or such conventions as disarmament conventions) dependent on a reciprocal or corresponding performance by other parties.[49]

Finally, it should be noted that, in its advisory opinion in the 'Namibia (South West Africa)' case, the majority opinion cited the definition of material breach set out in Article 60 of the Vienna Convention and noted that General Assembly resolution 2145 (XXI) had determined that both forms of material breach (i.e. repudiation of the treaty and violation of a provision essential to the accomplishment of the object or purpose of the treaty) had occurred in this case.[50] As against this, Judge Fitzmaurice, in his dissenting opinion, points out that the justification for the revocation of the mandate which the Court finds in Article 60(3)(a) of the Vienna Convention is quite misplaced, since the South African attitude was in no sense equivalent to a disavowal of the mandate—'to deny the existence of an obligation is *ex hypothesi* not the same as to repudiate it'.[51]

3 'REBUS SIC STANTIBUS'

All international lawyers are aware of the pitfalls surrounding the application of the *clausula rebus sic stantibus* and the controversies which have raged as to its admissibility as a ground for the unilateral denunciation or termination of a treaty.[52] The concept that (whether by way of an implied term or otherwise) a treaty may become inapplicable by reason of a fundamental change in circumstances obviously presents serious dangers to the security of treaties. The *rebus* doctrine fell into serious disrepute during the inter-war

[49] Fitzmaurice, '*Ex injuria non oritur jus*', 92 *Recueil des Cours* (1957), pp. 125–6.

[50] *I.C.J. Reports* (1971), p. 47.

[51] *Loc. cit.*, p. 300.

[52] See Hill, *The Doctrine of Rebus Sic Stantibus in International Law* (1934), *passim*; and, for a more recent study, Lissitzyn, 'Treaties and changed circumstances (*rebus sic stantibus*)', 61 *A.J.I.L.* (1967), pp. 895–922.

period, largely as a result of its indiscriminate invocation by States in the period before 1914 to escape from inconvenient treaty obligations.[53] It has never been applied *eo nomine* by the International Court of Justice or its predecessors. Indeed, in the 'Free Zones' case the Permanent Court of International Justice expressly reserved its position, observing that it was not necessary for the Court to consider 'any of the questions of principle which arise in connection with the theory of the lapse of treaties by reason of change of circumstances, such as the extent to which the theory can be regarded as constituting a rule of international law [and] the occasions on which and the method by which effect can be given to the theory if recognised'.[54]

Against this background, the Commission approached the formulation of a text on *rebus sic stantibus* with considerable caution. After extensive debate, they decided to formulate it in negative terms, declaring that a fundamental change of circumstances which had occurred with regard to those existing at the time of the conclusion of a treaty might not be invoked as a ground for terminating or withdrawing from the treaty unless two conditions were met:

(*a*) The existence of those circumstances constituted an essential basis of the consent of the parties to be bound by the treaty; *and*

(*b*) The effect of the change was radically to transform the scope of obligations still to be performed under the treaty.

To this the Commission proposed two exceptions:

(*a*) A fundamental change of circumstances could not be invoked as a ground for terminating or withdrawing from a treaty establishing a boundary.

(*b*) A fundamental change of circumstances could not be invoked if it was the result of a breach by the invoking party either of the treaty or of a different international obligation owed to the other parties to the treaty.

53 Garner, 'The doctrine of *rebus sic stantibus* and the termination of Treaties', 21 *A.J.I.L.* (1927), p. 509.

54 P.C.I.J., Series A/B, No. 46 (1932), pp. 156–8.

There was a lengthy debate at the conference on the Commission's proposals, which emerged at the end relatively unscathed. Taking up a suggestion which had been made by Lissitzyn,[55] the Canadian delegation proposed that, in circumstances where a party may invoke a fundamental change of circumstances as a ground for terminating or withdrawing from a treaty, it may also invoke that change as a ground for suspending the operation of the treaty; this proposal was adopted by the conference, and is now reflected in paragraph 3 of Article 62.

Some interesting points were made in the course of the debate. In the first place, it was suggested, and not denied, that a State would not be entitled to invoke its own acts or omissions as amounting to a fundamental change of circumstances giving rise to the operation of Article 62.[56] Attention was also directed to the view expressed by some members of the Commission, and recorded in the commentary to the Commission's proposal, that 'a subjective change in the attitude or policy of a Government could never be invoked as a ground for terminating, withdrawing from or suspending the operation of a treaty'.[57] As regards the asserted exception to this principle in the case of a treaty of alliance, where it was said that a radical change of political alignment by the government of a country might make it unacceptable, *from the point of view of both parties*, to continue the treaty, some delegations expressed the view that this was not a case for the operation of the principle *rebus sic stantibus* but rather for the application of the concept that a right of unilateral denunciation might be implied from the character of the treaty.[58] Other delegations were of opinion that a change in government policy should in no event be invoked as a ground for unilaterally terminating a treaty.[59]

Concern was expressed by several delegations (notably the delegations of Afghanistan and Syria) about the Commission's proposals to preclude invocation of fundamental change of circumstances in the case of a treaty establishing a boundary, but a proposal to delete what is now paragraph 2(a) of Article 62 was not pressed to a vote.

[55] *Loc. cit.*, p. 916.
[56] *Official Records, First Session*, 63rd meeting (Vallat).
[57] 1966 I.L.C. Reports, p. 87.
[58] *Official Records, First Session*, 63rd meeting (Vallat).
[59] *Loc. cit.*, 64th meeting (Harry).

VII CONCLUSIONS

I cannot conclude this brief survey of the various grounds for the invalidity, termination and suspension of operation of treaties without making a few critical observations. Few would quarrel with the view that the vagueness of the language employed in formulating this series of articles presents a potential danger to the stability of treaty relations. This is certainly true of the provisions relating to error, fraud and corruption, and even more true of the provisions concerning coercion of a State by the threat or use of force and *rebus sic stantibus*. O'Connell is of opinion that the Convention rules on coercion constitute 'a blank cheque to States seeking escape from inconvenient treaty commitments entered into in moments of political subordinacy to other Powers'.[60] Lissitzyn is highly critical of the ambiguities residing in such expressions as 'fundamental change', 'not foreseen by the parties', 'an essential basis of the consent of the parties' and 'radically to transform the extent of obligation' as used in Article 62 concerning the doctrine *rebus sic stantibus*.[61] Deleau regards the series of articles on error, fraud, corruption and coercion exercised against the representative of a State as being open to serious question:

> En effet, ces dispositions constituent une transposition assez discutable de la théorie des vices du consentement du droit interne des contrats dans le domaine des traités internationaux, et surtout formulent des hypothèses incertaines, subjectives et indéfiniment extensibles.[62]

Serious attempts were made at the conference to remove some of the ambiguities and uncertainties inherent in this series of articles, but most of the proposals designed to circumscribe the application of the various grounds of invalidity and termination of treaties met with strong resistance and were defeated on a vote. The Afro-Asian majority were extremely reluctant to countenance any material departure from the texts proposed by the Commission, particularly if it could be represented that the change was designed to keep in being so-called 'unequal' treaties.

[60] *Op. cit.*, p. 240.

[61] *Loc. cit.*, p. 914.

[62] Deleau, 'Les Positions françaises à la conférence de Vienne sur le droit des traités', 15 *Annuaire Français de Droit International* (1969), p. 13.

Against this background, and because all serious endeavours to improve the substantive content of this series of articles were unavailing, those delegations primarily concerned to uphold the sanctity of the principle *pacta sunt servanda* concentrated their efforts on seeking to establish a built-in system of automatically available procedures for the settlement of disputes arising out of the interpretation and application of Part V of the Convention. The establishment of such a system was rendered all the more necessary by the decision of the conference to accord recognition to the much-disputed concept that conflict with a peremptory norm of general international law from which no derogation is permitted (i.e. a norm of *jus cogens*) will render a treaty null and void. I propose to discuss these two issues in my next, and concluding, chapter, and also to present a few general thoughts on the Convention as a whole.

CHAPTER V

JUS COGENS AND THE SETTLEMENT OF DISPUTES

I *JUS COGENS*

The concept that a treaty concluded in violation of a norm of *jus cogens* is null and void is highly controversial. Any analysis of the concept requires an investigation into the relevance in international law of private law analogies and into the extent to which, if at all, there exists an objective notion of international public policy consisting of legal rules from which States are not permitted to derogate by way of international agreement.

But first, you may ask, what is *jus cogens*? Suy defines it as 'the body of those general rules of law whose non-observance may affect the very essence of the legal system to which they belong to such an extent that the subject of law may not, under pain of absolute nullity, depart from them in virtue of particular agreements'.[1] From this definition it will be noted that the concept of *jus cogens* is wholly general in nature and applicable to any system of law. It is not a concept which has been specially developed within the framework of public international law; on the contrary, it derives from, and is deeply embedded in, particular systems of private law.

The origin of the notion of *jus cogens* has been traced to Roman law. The maxim *jus publicum privatorum pactis mutari non potest* is to be found in the *Digest*.[2] The *jus publicum* was to be understood in a wide sense as embracing not only public law in the strict sense (that is to say, the law governing relations between individuals and the State) but also rules from which individuals were not permitted to depart by virtue of particular agreements.

The pervading influence of this general notion can be recognised by the development of such concepts as *ordre public* and *öffentliche Ordnung* in French and German law respectively, and by the gradual establishment in common law jurisdictions of the principle

[1] *Op. cit.*, p. 18.

[2] Digest II, 14, 38.

that certain types of contract are, by their very nature, injurious to society and therefore contrary to public policy. The genesis of this principle in English law can be traced back to Elizabethan times, although it was only in the eighteenth century that its foundations were effectively laid in a series of decisions proclaiming, in somewhat vague and indeterminate language, the nullity of contracts injurious to the public good or *contra bonos mores*.[3]

It will, then, be seen that every developed national system of law has devised its own concept of public policy. In civil law jurisdictions the notion of *ordre public* is essentially variable and relative, evolving in accordance with the political, social and economic circumstances of the time.[4] In English law it is less variable; certain defined heads of public policy have been established by the courts, and although these heads can be moulded to fit the new conditions of a changing world, it is rarely possible for the courts to establish new heads of public policy.[5]

Thus there has gradually evolved over the years, in practically all systems of municipal law, the principle that the will of the parties to conclude contracts is not unfettered but is subject to certain restraints essential to the continued existence of an ordered society. What the nature of these restraints is will vary according to the political, economic or social climate in the country concerned. Certain restraints may be imposed by statute, others may have been developed by the jurisprudence of the courts. So far as restraints imposed by statute are concerned, political and economic factors may lead to the imposition of new controls on the freedom of individuals to contract; thus, in England, the Resale Prices Act, 1964, rendered void (subject to an exemption procedure) any term or condition of a contract for the sale of goods by a supplier to a dealer in so far as it provided for the establishment of minimum prices for the resale of the goods.

Notwithstanding the close connection between *jus cogens* and public policy, the two concepts do not entirely coincide,[6] at least if

[3] Cheshire and Fifoot, *Law of Contract*, eighth edition (1972), pp. 318–25.

[4] Suy, *op. cit.*, p. 20.

[5] Janson *v.* Driefontein Consolidated Mines Ltd [1902] A.C. 484, at p. 492; Fender *v.* St John-Mildmay [1938] A.C. 1, at p. 40; see, however, McCardie J. in Naylor Benzon Ltd *v.* Krainische Ind. Ges. [1918] 1 K.B. 331, at p. 349, and Shaw *v.* Director of Public Prosecutions [1962] A.C. 220.

[6] Schwelb, 'Some aspects of international *jus cogens* as formulated by the International Law Commission', 61 *A.J.I.L.* (1967), p. 948.

public policy is conceived of in the narrower sense as being confined to the circumstances in which municipal courts will refuse to enforce a contract. *Jus cogens* is the sum of absolute, ordering, prohibiting municipal law prescriptions, in contrast to the *jus dispositivum*, that is to say, legal prescriptions which can, and do, yield to the will of the parties.

But of what relevance, you may ask, is this indeterminate concept to the development of international law? Does international law know—has it ever known—any corresponding notion of a superior order of legal prescriptions from which States are not free to derogate by treaty? The use of the phrase 'superior order' must ring a bell. Do we not begin to discern the outlines of the familiar doctrinal dispute between the naturalist and positivist schools? It will be recalled that long before Grotius it was generally accepted that, above the positive law grounded in custom and the practice of States, there was in existence another law rooted in human reason and deriving its force from theological and philosophical doctrine—the Law of Nature.[7] Grotius distinguished between the *jus gentium* (the customary law of nations, which he styled 'voluntary law') and the *jus naturae* (the natural law of nations), assigning a proper place to each. To the naturalists, the Law of Nature was hierarchically superior to the voluntary law—no State was at liberty to disregard the Law of Nature; the more extreme proponents of the naturalist school, such as Pufendorf, even denied the existence of any voluntary or positive law of nations outside the Law of Nature.

As a reaction against the theoretical and, at times, dogmatic approach of the naturalists, there began to develop, in the eighteenth century, a school of jurists, led by Bynkershoek, Moser and Martens, who laid increasing stress on the part played by custom and treaties in the development of positive international law. They did not wholly deny the role of natural law in filling gaps, but their emphasis on the constituent elements of positive international law gave them the title 'positivists'.

The predominance of the positivist school of jurists in the late nineteenth and early twentieth centuries led to a certain reaction in the inter-war years. The great contribution of the positivist school was to concentrate attention on State practice as a determining factor in the development of international law; but the more extreme adherents of the positivist school carried matters to excess

[7] Oppenheim, *International Law*, eighth edition (1955), vol. 1, p. 93.

when they equated positivism with exaggerated notions of State sovereignty by insisting that the will of States constituted the only valid source of international law.

Current discussion of the concept of *jus cogens* re-echoes some of the great debates of the past between naturalists and positivists, though with a more modern flavour. There has been a vast outpouring of studies on the concept of *jus cogens* in international law, stimulated in large measure by the activities of the International Law Commission on the law of treaties.[8] The current debate turns in large measure on the extent to which one can make use of private law analogies and on the evidence for the recognition of a rule in international law which restricts the liberty of States to conclude treaties regardless of their content.

Let us examine first the usefulness in this sphere of private law analogies. No one would deny the existence in municipal legal systems of a concept of public policy comparable to, even if not synonymous with, *jus cogens*. But, interestingly, Lauterpacht, writing in 1927 about the application of private law analogies to treaties, nowhere makes mention of any concept of *jus cogens* as a restriction upon the power of States to conclude treaties, notwithstanding his express statement that 'the legal nature of private law contracts and international law treaties is essentially the same'.[9] He discusses in detail such matters as duress and *rebus sic stantibus*, where the analogy between contracts and treaties tends to fall down, and he acknowledges the vitiating effect of fraud and error in relation to treaties;[10] but he is singularly silent on what one would

[8] See articles by Suy and Schwarzenberger in *The Concept of Jus Cogens in International Law*; Verdross, '*Jus dispositivum* and *jus cogens* in international law', 60 *A.J.I.L.* (1966), pp. 55–63; Schwelb, *loc. cit.*, pp. 946–75; Virally, 'Réflexions sur le *jus cogens*', 12 *Annuaire Français de Droit International* (1966), pp. 1–29; Schwarzenberger, *International Law and Order* (1971), pp. 27–56; Marek, 'Contribution a l'étude du *jus cogens* en droit international' in *Hommage à Paul Guggenheim* (1968), pp. 426–59; Scheuner, 'Conflict of treaty provisions with a peremptory norm of general international law and its consequences', *Zeitschrift für ausländisches öffentliches Recht und Völkerrecht* (1967), pp. 520–532; Nisot, 'Le Concept de *jus cogens* par rapport au droit international', *Revue Belge de Droit International* (1968), pp. 1–7; Barberis, 'La Liberté de traiter des états et le *jus cogens*', *Z.a.o.R.V.* (1970), pp. 19–45; de Visscher, 'Positivisme et *jus cogens*', 75 *Revue Générale de Droit International Public* (1971), Part 1, pp. 5–11.

[9] *Private Law Sources and Analogies of International Law* (1927), p. 156.

[10] *Ibid.*, p. 176.

assume to be a more pertinent analogy between contracts and treaties —namely, the extent to which the parties are free to determine the content of their agreement.

In a much more recent study Marek points out some of the conditions for the effective application in domestic law of notions of public policy or *ordre public*—conditions which do not exist in the present state of international society or which exist only in a very rudimentary form. First, she reminds us that, in any developed national legal system, there is a recognised hierarchy of legal norms —the constitution, statutes, regulations, judicial decisions and administrative acts. Second, she recalls that, within national legal systems, the subjects of the law do not, in general, have capacity to lay down general rules: this is the exclusive responsibility of the legislator. Third, she draws attention to the fact that, in municipal law, legal rights enjoyed by subjects of the law (i.e. individuals) are in general heteronomous (that is to say, subject to external and objective law) rather than autonomous (that is to say, created by the subjects of the law themselves). Fourth, she mentions that the effective limitation of freedom to contract in municipal law results from the sanctions which State organs (including the courts) can impose upon any breach of that limitation. Fifth and finally, she points to the existence, in all municipal law systems, of courts endowed with effective, permanent and obligatory jurisdiction to define and crystallise the limits within which the principle of freedom of contract subject to the law can operate.[11]

These necessary conditions for the application of legal rules restricting the freedom of parties to determine the content of their agreements exist only in a very fragmentary and rudimentary form in international law. In contrast to the position in developed municipal legal systems, international law has no regular and defined hierarchy of norms, at any rate if one ignores the metaphysical search for the *Grundnorm* as the source for the binding force of international law in general. As the subjects of international law are, generally speaking, States, there is no independent legislator, so that there is in reality no distinction, as there is in municipal law, between the parties to a contract, who can create only individual rights between themselves, and the legislator who can lay down general rules. In international law, there are, of course, no centralised sanctions for the breach of limitations imposed by law, save

[11] Marek, *loc cit.*, pp. 429–32.

where sanctions may be imposed under the U.N. Charter, and equally no system of compulsory jurisdiction enabling a judicial organ to determine questions concerning the legality of treaties.

Thus the analogies from private law sources do not seem very apt to warrant the conclusion that there exist, in present-day international law, certain peremptory norms from which States cannot derogate by treaty. But this by no means concludes the analysis. Indeed, it is only the beginning. If the private law analogies do not afford much guidance, can one deduce the existence of *jus cogens* in international law from other sources?

Admitting that international law is still primitive law in the sense that it lacks certain of the attributes of developed municipal legal systems, is one forced to the conclusion that this very 'primitiveness' excludes the possibility of restraints upon the capacity of States to conclude treaties regardless of their content? Schwarzenberger would respond in the affirmative; after an examination of the principles of customary international law, he concludes that 'the evidence of international law on the level of *unorganised* international society fails to bear out any claim for the existence of international *jus cogens*'.[12] The majority of jurists, however conscious they may be of the dangers which are presented to the security of treaties by recognition of so vague and uncertain a concept, would hesitate to go so far. They would hesitate the more if they were to follow the advice given by one of my mentors in international law, the late Sir Eric Beckett, who was accustomed to test the validity of any proposition by applying it to the extreme case and seeing whether it held good for that.[13]

Testing at its limits the proposition that States are free to conclude treaties regardless of their content, one can enquire whether it would be possible for States A and B to conclude a treaty declaring that all treaties which they had previously concluded, or would conclude in the future, were not binding. Such a treaty, in open violation of the principle *pacta sunt servanda*, poses a logical conundrum, for its validity would appear to depend on the very norm which it purports to abolish.[14] Let me take another example. Would it be possible for States A and B, by treaty, to agree to commit an

[12] *International Law and Order*, p. 51.

[13] Fitzmaurice and Vallat, 'Sir (William) Eric Beckett, K.C.M.G., Q.C. (1896–1966): an appreciation', 17 *I.C.L.Q.* (1968), p. 288.

[14] Cf. Marek, *loc cit.*, 448.

act of aggression on a specified date against State C? The answer is self-evidently in the negative; the stipulation is a nullity, since its execution would involve a criminal act, the planning, preparation, initiation or waging of a war of aggression having been declared to be an international crime against the peace.[15]

Here we come close to the heart of the matter, since acceptance of the view that there are certain norms of international law of so fundamental a character that it is legally impermissible to derogate from them by treaty involves acceptance in principle of the operation of *jus cogens* in international law. The question then poses itself: what is the content of *jus cogens*?

Before seeking to analyse the content of *jus cogens*, it would be as well to examine the doctrinal evidence, and the evidence of State practice, in favour of the concept that violation of a norm of *jus cogens* will render a treaty null and void.

I DOCTRINAL EVIDENCE

Suy has given us an extended analysis of the views of eminent writers on this point. He finds the greatest support for the existence of *jus cogens* in international law among German, Swiss and Austrian publicists. Von der Heydte,[16] Verdross,[17] Dahm,[18] Berber[19] and Guggenheim,[20] while acknowledging that the majority of rules of international law are dispositive in character, proclaim

[15] Article 6(a) of the Charter of the International Military Tribunal (Treaty Series, No. 27 (1946)); the Nuremberg principles were endorsed in General Assembly resolution 95 (I) of 11 December 1946. See also General Assembly resolution 2625 (XXV), covering the Declaration on Principles of International Law concerning Friendly Relations and Co-operation among States.

[16] *Völkerrecht* (1958), vol. I, p. 23.

[17] *Völkerrecht*, fifth edition (1964), p. 130; see also *id.*, 'Forbidden treaties in international law', 31 *A.J.I.L.* (1937), pp. 571–7, and 60 *A.J.I.L.* (1966), pp. 55–63.

[18] *Völkerrecht*, vol. I (1958), pp. 6, 17, and vol. III (1961), p. 140.

[19] *Lehrbuch des Völkerrechts*, vol. I (1960), p. 439.

[20] Note on 'Verträge' in Strupp and Schlochauer, *Wörterbuch des Völkerrechts*, vol. 3 (1962), p. 531. But note that Guggenheim had earlier expressed the view that 'international law accordingly admits that a treaty may have any content whatsoever, without limitations or restrictions of any kind, and that anything can be made the subject of a treaty': *Traité de Droit International Public*, vol. I (1953), p. 57.

the existence of certain rules of so fundamental a character that, exceptionally, treaties concluded in violation of them are void.

French writers have traditionally been more reserved. Rousseau is highly sceptical about the notion of *jus cogens*. He points out that, in international law, by contrast with the position in domestic law, 'the notion of a public policy limiting the autonomy of the will of the State is practically non-existent, because of the individualistic and voluntarist structure of the international community'; the notion of a treaty with an illegal object is, for him, without any practical interest, the examples given being purely academic.[21] Fauchille, on the other hand, admits the possibility of a hierarchy of norms, and avows that treaties must have a lawful object.[22] Sibert[23] and Cavaré[24] likewise appear to concede that there are limits to the freedom of States to conclude treaties, and that certain types of treaty, such as a treaty legalising piracy or slavery, are unlawful.

English and American writers have expressed a wide range of views on this matter. McNair notes that in every civilised communiy there are some rules of law and some principles of morality which individuals are not permitted by law to ignore, or to modify, by their agreements; applying this conception to international law, he accepts that among the rules of customary international law which stand in a higher category and which cannot be set aside or modified by contracting States are 'rules which have been accepted, either expressly by treaty or tacitly by custom, as being necessary to protect the public interest of the society of States or to maintain the standards of public morality recognised by them'.[25] Brownlie also appears to admit, although with some hesitation, the existence of *jus cogens*, conceding that there is more authority for the category of *jus cogens* than for its particular content.[26] Jenks is even more hesitant: although in principle he favours the notion of an international public policy, he takes the view that the *jus dispositivum* consisting of treaty stipulations agreed between the parties is not generally regarded as being governed by any *jus cogens* which

[21] *Principes Généraux du Droit International Public*, vol. I, pp. 341–2.

[22] *Traité de Droit International Public*, vol. I, Part 3 (1926), p. 300.

[23] *Ibid.* (1951), p. 212.

[24] *Droit International Public Positif*, second edition (1962), vol. II, p. 69.

[25] *Op. cit.*, pp. 214–15.

[26] *Principles of Public International Law* (1966), pp. 417–18; cf. also *International Law and the Use of Force by States* (1961), p. 409.

negotiators of a treaty can ignore at their peril, although he does not exclude the possibility of a development of *jus cogens* in this sense.[27] Schwarzenberger, as we have seen, is the most sceptical of all; he denies the existence of *jus cogens* on the level of unorganised international society and stigmatises the draft article on *jus cogens* submitted by the Commission as being 'perfectly adapted to the idiosyncrasies of a hypocritical age'.[28]

Finally, we come to the views advanced by the Special Rapporteurs on the Law of Treaties. Lauterpacht, in his 'First Report on the Law of Treaties', proposed a provision in the following terms:

> A treaty, or any of its provisions, is void if its performance involves an act which is illegal under international law and if it is declared so to be by the International Court of Justice.[29]

It should be noted that the emphasis is placed here upon *acts* which are illegal under international law and that, already, an indivisible link is posited between the proclamation of the principle and its application by an international tribunal. Lauterpacht makes it clear, in his commentary, that States are free to modify by treaty, *as between themselves,* rules of customary international law so long as the treaty does not affect the rights of third States; in his view, the test whether the object of the treaty is illegal and whether the treaty is void for that reason 'is not inconsistency with customary international law pure and simple, but inconsistency with such overriding principles of international law which may be regarded as constituting international public policy'.

Fitzmaurice, in his 'Third Report on the Law of Treaties', was also prepared to envisage that conflict with a norm of *jus cogens* will invalidate a treaty. Article 16(2) of the Fitzmaurice draft reads as follows:

> It is essential to the validity of a treaty that it should be in conformity with or not contravene or that its execution should not involve an infraction of those principles and rules of international law which are in the nature of *jus cogens.*

In his commentary to Article 17, Fitzmaurice points out that the majority of the rules of international law are *jus dispositivum* and

[27] *The Prospects of International Adjudication* (1964), p. 504, and pp. 458–60.
[28] *International Law and Order,* p. 50.
[29] A/CN.4/63 of 24 March 1953.

that it is 'only as regards rules of international law having a kind of absolute and non-rejectable character (which admit of no option) that the question of the illegality and invalidity of a treaty inconsistent with them can arise'. He cites as examples a bilateral treaty to wage a war of aggression against a third State and a bilateral treaty whereby the two States agree not to take any prisoners of war, and to execute all captured personnel, during future hostilities between them.

2 EVIDENCE OF STATE PRACTICE

If there is a preponderant body of opinion among publicists in favour of the existence of a concept of *jus cogens* in international law, it must be admitted that evidence of its application (or even consideration) by international tribunals or in international practice is sparse.

So far as international tribunals are concerned, the only reference to the concept in the jurisprudence of the Permanent Court of International Justice and the International Court of Justice are to be found in individual or dissenting judgments. The most striking is Judge Schücking's dissent in the 'Oscar Chinn' case, where, with reference to Article 20 of the Covenant of the League of Nations, he states:

> . . . I can hardly believe that the League of Nations would have already embarked on the codification of international law if it were not possible even today to create a *jus cogens* the effect of which would be that, once States have agreed on certain rules of law, and have also given an undertaking that these rules may not be altered by some of their number, any act adopted in contravention of that undertaking would be automatically void.[30]

In the 'Wimbledon' case, Judge Schücking's dissent was again based in part on the postulated existence of rules of *jus cogens* from which States cannot derogate by treaty. It will be recalled that the question at issue was whether Germany, as a neutral in the hostilities between Poland and the Soviet Union in 1921, was obliged, by virtue of Article 380 of the Treaty of Versailles, to permit contraband for Poland to pass through the Kiel Canal. In dissenting from the Court's view that Germany was so obliged, Judge Schücking

[30] P.C.I.J., Series A/B, No .63, pp. 149–50.

expressed the view that the duties of a neutral must take precedence over treaty obligations and that it is impossible to undertake by treaty a contractual obligation to perform acts which would violate rights of third parties.[31]

The individual opinions of Judge Anzilotti[32] in the 'Austro-German customs regime' case and of Judge Moreno Quintana[33] in the 'Guardianship of infants' case have also been cited as evidence of a recognition by individual judges of the existence of a concept of *jus cogens* in international law. It is doubtful, however, whether these isolated *dicta* add up to very much.

More interesting is a recent case before the Bundesverfassungsgericht in the Federal Republic of Germany. The German Equalisation of Burdens Law of 1952 had imposed certain taxes for the purpose of raising revenue to defray the costs of compensation for losses suffered by persons expelled from former German territories in the East and by war victims of various designated categories. A Convention between the Federal Republic and Switzerland provided that this law should apply to Swiss nationals to the extent that it applied to nationals of the most favoured nation. A Swiss company claimed that the German–Swiss Convention violated an asserted rule of customary international law to the effect that resort to aliens for the purpose of defraying expenditures resulting from the consequences of a war is not permissible. The Federal Constitutional Court appears to have interpreted this as an argument that the asserted rule of customary international law was *jus cogens* and disposed of the point as follows:

> Only a few elementary mandates may be considered to be rules of customary international law which cannot be stipulated away by treaty. The quality of such peremptory norms may be attributed only to such legal rules as are firmly rooted in the legal conviction of the community of nations and are indispensable to the existence of the law of nations as an international legal order, and the observance of which can be required by all members of the international community. The rule that no resort may be had to aliens for the defrayal of expenditure resulting from war consequences certainly does not fall into this class of peremptory rules of international law.[34]

---

[31] P.C.I.J., Series A, No. 1, p. 47.

[32] P.C.I.J., Series A/B, No. 41, p. 64.

[33] *I.C.J. Reports* (1958), pp. 106–7.

[34] See Riesenfeld, 'Jus dispositivum and jus cogens in international law in

So far as State practice is concerned, the allegation has been made before certain organs of the United Nations (in particular, the Security Council) that Article IV of the Treaty of Guarantee between Cyprus, on the one hand, and Greece, Turkey and the United Kingdom, on the other hand, is invalid in so far as it might be interpreted to authorise the unilateral intervention of any of the guaranteeing powers in Cyprus. This allegation was contested on the grounds that the action reserved to the guaranteeing powers as provided for in Article IV(2) of the Treaty of Guarantee could be resorted to only in the event of a breach of the provisions of the treaty, i.e. in circumstances in which there was a threat to the independence, territorial integrity or security of the Republic of Cyprus as established by the basic articles of its constitution.[35]

3 CONTENT OF 'JUS COGENS'

It now remains to consider the most controversial aspect of them all: if, on the balance of conflicting considerations, one is constrained to admit the existence of *jus cogens* in international law, what is its content? What are these peremptory norms of general international law from which States are not permitted to derogate by treaty?

Let us begin by taking the more obvious candidates. I have already discussed the extreme case of a treaty which purports to abolish both retrospectively and prospectively the rule *pacta sunt servanda* in relations between the contracting parties; however improbable such a treaty may be, it is difficult to see how its validity could be sustained. But leaving aside treaties whose object and purpose is to deny the fundamental principle underlying the law of treaties itself, what other categories of treaty could be regarded as being inconsistent with rules of *jus cogens*?

The Commission's commentary gives three examples:

(*a*) A treaty contemplating an unlawful use of force contrary to the principles of the Charter.

(*b*) A treaty contemplating the performance of any other act criminal under international law.

---

the light of a recent decision of the German Supreme Constitutional Court', 60 *A.J.I.L.* (1966), pp. 511–15.

[35] *Repertoire of the Practice of the Security Council*, Supplement 1964–5, pp. 201, 221; see also Schwelb, *loc. cit.*, pp. 952–3.

(*c*) A treaty contemplating or conniving at the commission of acts, such as trade in slaves, piracy or genocide, in the suppression of which every State is called upon to co-operate.

There would be little disposition among jurists to deny the nullity of a treaty contemplating an unlawful use of force contrary to the principles of the Charter; but, given the pervasive influence of the modern propaganda machine designed to stand everything on its head, it is of course necessary to distinguish a treaty of this nature from a perfectly valid treaty for the organisation of collective self-defence in the event of an armed attack or the threat of an armed attack.

The second example given by the Commission in part overlaps the first, since a treaty between States A and B for the initiation of a war of aggression against State C would, as already indicated, fall foul of both prohibitions. But the second example would presumably also cover the other instance cited by Fitzmaurice—that is to say, a treaty whereby two States agree not to take any prisoners of war, and to execute all captured personnel, during future hostilities between them. In this connection, Schwelb aptly reminds us that the four Geneva Conventions of 1949 on the Protection of War Victims all contain denunciation clauses providing that each of the parties shall be at liberty to denounce the Conventions; but the denunciation clauses specifically state that denunciation 'shall in no way impair the obligations which the parties to the conflict shall remain bound to fulfil by virtue of the principles of the law of nations, as they result from the usages established among civilised peoples, from the laws of humanity and the dictates of the public conscience'. Schwelb concludes that this is a reference to something akin to *jus cogens*, since, if a single State cannot release itself from their provisions by the act of denouncing the Conventions, it appears to follow that two or more States cannot derogate from these principles by agreements among themselves.[36] In this he is probably right, given the particular content of the Geneva Conventions. But it does not follow that the inclusion of such a provision in the denunciation clause of another Convention would constitute conclusive evidence of the *jus cogens* character of the rules embodied in that Convention, since its purpose may be simply to preserve the operation of the rules as rules of customary international law. In

[36] *Loc. cit.*, pp. 956–7.

the final analysis, it is the *content* of the rules which will be decisive in the determination of whether or not they have the attributes of *jus cogens*.

The third example given by the Commission opens up the flood-gates of controversy. The majority of jurists would no doubt go along with the Commission in asserting that the rules prohibiting trade in slaves, piracy or genocide have become norms of *jus cogens* from which States are not free to derogate by treaty.[37] But a word of caution is necessary here. It is right to recall that general multi-lateral Conventions (even those recently concluded) which prohibit or outlaw slavery and the slave trade and genocide contain normal denunciation clauses.[38] If a State can release itself easily from the conventional obligations it has undertaken in these fields, can it be said that the prohibitions are in the nature of *jus cogens*? Of course, it may be said that the rule prohibiting slavery and the slave trade and the rule prohibiting genocide are rules of general international law which apply independently of the treaties embodying them. More to the point, it is clear that a treaty between two member States of the United Nations contemplating genocide or slavery would be wholly contrary to Articles 55 and 56 of the Charter and would therefore be unenforceable by virtue of Article 103, which provides that, in the event of conflict between the obligations of member States under the Charter and obligations under any other international agreement, Charter obligations prevail. The explana-tion for the existence of normal denunciation clauses in general multilateral Conventions which contain asserted norms of *jus cogens* is, as Schwelb indicates, that 'the idea of international *jus cogens* has not yet penetrated into the day-to-day thinking and action of governments'.[39]

Other examples have been suggested. Barberis mentions treaties contrary to the rules of international law relating to the white slave traffic.[40] Verdross goes much wider in asserting that 'all rules of general international law created for a humanitarian purpose' con-stitute *jus cogens*.[41] Apart from the difficulty of delimiting what is and what is not a humanitarian purpose, this seems to go much too

[37] Barberis, *loc. cit.*, pp. 34–5: Verdross, 60 *A.J.I.L.* (1966), p. 59.
[38] Schwelb, *loc. cit.*, p. 953.
[39] *Loc. cit.*, p. 956.
[40] *Loc. cit.*, p. 35.
[41] 60 *A.J.I.L.* (1966), p. 59.

far. It implies that all human rights provisions contained in international treaties have the character of *jus cogens*. Given that even the United Nations Covenant on Civil and Political Rights is geared only towards 'achieving *progressively* the full realisation of the rights recognised in the present Covenant by all appropriate means',[42] it would be unwise to take at its face value the suggestion that *jus cogens* embraces all human rights provisions, despite the fact that, in the Commission's commentary, certain members are recorded as having given treaties violating human rights as an example of treaties which would contravene a rule of *jus cogens*.[43]

Marek, in an attempt to find an underlying principle, advances the superficially attractive proposition that a treaty violative of *jus cogens* is any treaty in which two or more States undertake to commit acts which would be illegal if committed by a single State.[44] But even this appears to go too wide; it would seem to exclude the possibility of *inter se* modification of a multilateral treaty, even although *inter se* modification is permissible under certain conditions.

4 'JUS COGENS' AND THE VIENNA CONVENTION

We have so far discussed the topic of *jus cogens* in the abstract. It remains to consider how *jus cogens* is dealt with in the Convention.

The Commission had proposed a draft article in the following terms:

> A treaty is void if it conflicts with a peremptory norm of general international law from which no derogation is permitted and which can be modified only by a subsequent norm of general international law having the same character.[45]

A lengthy debate in the conference brought forth a variety of views. Few, if any, delegations sought to deny entirely the concept of *jus cogens*, but a number of criticisms were directed against the wording of the Commission's proposal. First, it was maintained—particularly by the delegations of Chile and Mexico—that the wording was circular, in the sense that apparently a norm of *jus cogens* (from which no derogation by treaty was permissible) could be modified

[42] Article 2(1).
[43] 1966 I.L.C. Reports, p. 77.
[44] *Loc cit.*, p. 452.
[45] 1966 I.L.C. Reports, p. 75 (Article 50).

by a general multilateral treaty laying down new norms of *jus cogens*.[46] Second, it was argued that the analogy from private law concepts was misconceived, since, within the framework of international society, there was no acknowledged legislator competent to decree that a rule was of the character of public policy.[47] Third, and most persistently, it was emphasised that the Commission's draft did not provide any definition of *jus cogens* nor did it contain any test whereby norms of *jus cogens* could be identified. This last criticism was voiced by many delegations, particularly from Western countries.

Among the foremost proponents of *jus cogens* at the conference were the Eastern European delegations. Their views on its content reveal a marked imprecision. The representative of the Soviet Union characterised as having the nature of *jus cogens* 'such principles as non-aggression and non-interference in the internal affairs of States (*sic*), sovereign equality, national self-determination and other basic principles of contemporary international law and Articles 1 and 2 of the United Nations Charter'.[48] To the representative of Poland, the principles in Article 2 of the United Nations Charter formed part of *jus cogens*, as did 'the freedom on the high seas, the prohibition of slavery and genocide and some of the rules of land warfare'.[49] The Byellorussian delegate cited in this context 'the maintenance of peace among peoples, the struggle against colonial domination and the sovereignty of States';[50] and the Ukrainian delegate gave as examples of peremptory norms 'the universally recognised principles of international law prohibiting *inter alia* the use of force, unlawful war and colonialism'.[51] This vague catalogue of general principles only served to confirm the anxieties of other delegations that the concept of *jus cogens* might be utilised as a weapon to undermine the security of treaties. Accordingly, it is not surprising that a number of amendments were tabled which were designed to provide a test for the identification of norms of *jus cogens*.

The United States delegation proposed a two-part amendment. The first part (which was adopted by the conference) made it clear

46 *Official Records, First Session*, 52nd meeting (Barros and Suarez).
47 *Ibid.*, 53rd meeting (Miras).
48 *Ibid.*, 52nd meeting (Khlestov).
49 *Ibid.*, 53rd meeting (Nahlik).
50 *Ibid.*, 54th meeting (Kudryavtsev).
51 *Ibid.*, 56th meeting (Makarevich).

that the article applied only to a treaty which 'at the time of its conclusion' violated a norm of *jus cogens*. The Commission's commentary had already made it clear that the rule stated in the article was not intended to operate retroactively,[52] and this part of the United States amendment merely clarified the underlying meaning of the text. The second part of the United States amendment was designed to establish a test for the identification of norms of *jus cogens* by requiring that such a norm must be 'recognised in common by the national and regional legal systems of the world'. It was explained in support of this part of the amendment that it was based on the consideration that 'a rule of international law was only *jus cogens* if it was universal in character and endorsed by the international community as a whole'.[53]

Following the same line of thought, the delegations of Finland, Greece and Spain tabled a proposal requiring that a norm of *jus cogens* must be 'recognised by the international community' as a norm from which no derogation was permitted. In the view of the sponsors, the essential element of international *jus cogens* lay in the universality of its acceptance by the international community, and their proposal was designed to stress the notion of general consent.[54]

In the event, and after complicated procedural manœuvres,[55] the second part of the United States amendment was put to the vote and defeated, while the less stringent proposal by Finland, Greece and Spain was referred to the Drafting Committee. Further lengthy discussions took place in the Drafting Committee, which eventually reported out the text now appearing as Article 53 of the Convention. In introducing this new text, the chairman of the Drafting Committee stated:

> The Drafting Committee had decided that the amendment by Finland, Greece and Spain would clarify the text, and had therefore inserted the phrase 'a peremptory norm of general international law is a norm accepted and recognised by the international community of States as a whole'. Only the word 'recognised' was used in the Three-Power amendment, but the Drafting Committee had added the word 'accepted' because

[52] 1966 I.L.C. Reports, p. 77.

[53] *Official Records, First Session*, 52nd meeting (Sweeney).

[54] *Ibid.*, 52nd meeting (Evrigenis).

[55] See Neuhold, 'The 1968 session of the United Nations Conference on the Law of Treaties, 19 *Osterreichische Zeitschrift für öffentliches Recht* (1969), p. 86.

it was to be found, together with the word 'recognised' in Article 38 of the Statute of the International Court of Justice.[56]

Ambassador Yasseen further explained that by inserting the words 'as a whole' in Article 53, the Drafting Committee had wished to stress that there was no question of requiring a rule to be accepted and recognised as peremptory by all States; in other words, no individual State should have the right of veto in determining what were and what were not peremptory norms.

There is little doubt that the revised text reported out by the Drafting Committee and now embodied in Article 53 of the Convention constitutes an improvement on the text originally proposed by the Commission. There is now a criterion (however vague and shadowy it may be) for determining whether or not a particular rule of general international law constitutes a norm of *jus cogens*. The requirement that there must be acceptance and recognition of the peremptory nature of the norm by the international community of States as a whole does provide a degree of protection against abusive claims that particular treaties are null and void because they conflict with an asserted norm of *jus cogens* based upon a self-serving and tortured interpretation of pseudo-legal principles. Whether or not the changes made at the conference in the text of what is now Article 53 have 'discreetly defused this time-bomb in the edifice of the Vienna Convention', as Schwarzenberger claims,[57] may be a matter of dispute. It is clear at any rate that some do not think so. Deleau, in describing the French positions at the Vienna conference, expresses the concern voiced by the French delegation at the time that a State which has not, as it were, participated in the international community consensus may be obliged to accept as imperative a rule which it would not, for its part, have accepted and recognised as such.[58]

The improvements effected in the text of the Commission proposal at Vienna—that is to say, the explicit recognition of the non-retroactive character of the rule and the incorporation of a vague test for the identification of norms of *jus cogens*—would not by themselves have been sufficient to allay all the anxieties which had been expressed about the dangers to the security of treaties which

[56] *Official Records, First Session*, 80th meeting (Yasseen).
[57] *International Law and Order*, p. 53.
[58] *Loc. cit.*, p. 18.

might flow from the application of the principle that nullity attaches to any treaty concluded in violation of an existing norm of *jus cogens*. In the view of the overwhelming majority of Western delegations represented at the conference, supported on this issue by a number of Latin American and Afro-Asian delegations, additional safeguards were essential. In particular, it was made crystal clear that the attitude of many delegations towards the series of articles on invalidity, and particularly the article on *jus cogens*, would be decisively influenced by the outcome of the debate at the conference on proposals to strengthen the machinery for the settlement of disputes arising in connection with the interpretation and application of Part V of the Convention.

5 INTERIM CONCLUSIONS ON 'JUS COGENS'

What conclusions can we draw so far from this analysis of the controversy surrounding the admissibility and application of the concept of *jus cogens* in international law? Perhaps one should stress at the outset that the 'great debate' on this issue involves taking a view on some of the fundamental and basic underpinnings of international law in general. It is no accident that some of the more vigorous Western proponents of *jus cogens* base their case largely upon private law analogies and upon concepts deriving from natural law. It is, equally, no accident that those who deny the existence of *jus cogens* found their denial in part upon considerations relating to State sovereignty and independence,[59] and in part upon an analysis of the evidence of State practice;[60] these are, of course, some of the hallmarks of the positivist approach. As de Visscher rightly points out, the controversy surrounding *jus cogens* constitutes a renewal, in different terms, of the ancient doctrinal dispute between naturalists and positivists.[61]

But there is a paradox here, particularly if one notes the enthusiasm of Soviet and other Eastern European publicists and official representatives for an extended application of the concept of *jus cogens* in international law. For those attached to Marxist-Leninist teachings there can be no place for any seed-bed of natural law in which *jus cogens* might take root. Equally, it might be thought un-

[59] Nisot, *Revue Belge de Droit International* (1968), pp. 1–2.
[60] Schwarzenberger, *International Law and Order*, pp. 29–48.
[61] 75 *Revue Générale de Droit International Public* (1971), Part 1, p. 11.

natural that Soviet representatives, traditionally supporting some of the more exaggerated notions of State sovereignty, should come down in favour of a concept which postulates the existence of a superior international legal order. This perhaps accounts for the emphasis put by Professor Tunkin on the argument that *jus cogens* is a *new* development in international law resulting from great developments on the political, technical, economic and cultural levels, together with the advent of massive destruction vehicles.[62] It may also account for the firm assertion of the Hungarian representative at the conference that *jus cogens* 'was not based on the theory of natural law but on the reality of the relations between States' and that the source of rules of *jus cogens* 'lay in the will of States'.[63] The suspicion must nevertheless remain that there is at the very least an element of opportunism in the attitude of some of the more enthusiastic proponents of *jus cogens*, given the doctrinal paradoxes noted above.

Whatever their doctrinal point of departure, the majority of jurists would no doubt willingly concede to the sceptics that there is little or no evidence in positive international law for the concept that nullity attaches to a treaty concluded in violation of *jus cogens*. But they would be constrained to admit that the validity of a treaty between two States to wage a war of aggression against a third State or to engage in acts of physical or armed force against a third State could not be upheld; and, having made this admission, they may be taken to have accepted the principle that there may exist norms of international law so fundamental to the maintenance of an international legal order that a treaty concluded in violation of them is a nullity.

Some (among whom may be counted your author) would be prepared to go this far, but would immediately wish to qualify this acceptance of the principle involved by sketching out the limits within which it may be operative in present-day international law. In the first place, they would insist that, in the present state of international society, the concept of an 'international legal order' of hierarchically superior norms binding all States is only just beginning to emerge. Ideological differences and disparities of wealth between the individual nation States which make up the international community, combined with the contrasts between the

[62] In *The Concept of Jus Cogens in International Law* (1967), p. 87.
[63] *Official Records, First Session,* 54th meeting (Bokor-Szegö.)

objectives sought by them, hinder the development of an overarching community consensus upon the content of *jus cogens*. Indeed, it is the existence of these very differences and disparities which constitute the principal danger implicit in an unqualified recognition of *jus cogens*; for it would be only too easy to postulate as a norm of *jus cogens* a principle which happened neatly to serve a particular ideological or economic goal. In the second place, they would test any assertion that a particular rule constitutes a norm of *jus cogens* by reference to the evidence for its acceptance as such by the international community as a whole, and they would require that the burden of proof should be discharged by those who allege the *jus cogens* character of the rule. Applying this test, and leaving aside the highly theoretical case of a treaty purporting to deny the application of the principle *pacta sunt servanda*, it would seem that sufficient evidence for ascribing the character of *jus cogens* to a rule of international law exists in relation to the rule which requires States to refrain in their international relations from the threat of force against the territorial integrity or political independence of any other State. There is ample evidence for the proposition that, subject to the necessary exceptions about the use of force in self-defence or under the authority of a competent organ of the United Nations or a regional agency acting in accordance with the Charter, the use of armed or physical force against the territorial integrity or political independence of any State is now prohibited. This proposition is so central to the existence of any international legal order of individual nation States (however nascent that international legal order may be) that it must be taken to have the character of *jus cogens*. Just as national legal systems begin to discard, at an early stage of their development, such concepts as 'trial by battle', so also must the international legal order be assumed now to deny any cover of legality to violations of the fundamental rule embodied in Article 2(4) of the Charter.

Beyond this, uncertainty begins, and one must tread with considerable caution. The dictates of logic, and overriding considerations of morality, would appear to require that one should characterise as *jus cogens* those rules which prohibit the slave trade and genocide; but the evidence is ambivalent, since the treaties which embody these prohibitions contain normal denunciation clauses. Of course, it may be argued that the presence or absence of normal denunciation clauses should not be taken as being decisive; denunciation clauses are regularly embodied in treaties for traditional, rather than practical, reasons. In any event, it is likely that the prohibitions may now be taken to form part of general international law binding all States regardless of whether they are parties to the treaties embodying them. The unenforceability of any treaty contemplating genocide or the slave trade is further assured by the fact that such a treaty would contravene the Charter of the United Nations, which prevails in the event of conflict.[64]

To sum up, there is a place for the concept of *jus cogens* in international law. Its growth and development will parallel the growth and development of an international legal order expressive of the consensus of the international community as a whole. Such an international legal order is, at present, inchoate, unformed and only just discernible. *Jus cogens* is neither Dr Jekyll nor Mr Hyde; but it has the potentialities of both. If it is invoked indiscriminately and to serve short-term political purposes, it could rapidly be destructive of confidence in the security of treaties; if it is developed with wisdom and restraint in the overall interest of the international community it could constitute a useful check upon the unbridled will of individual States.

II SETTLEMENT OF PART V DISPUTES

In the review of the various grounds of invalidity, termination and suspension of operation of treaties, I have, on several occasions, drawn attention to the importance attached by many States to the inclusion in the Convention of a satisfactory system for the settlement of disputes arising on the interpretation or application of this series of articles.

The Commission had proposed, in 1966, a draft article which in substance laid down certain procedural requirements which had to be fulfilled by States claiming that a treaty was invalid or alleging a ground for terminating, withdrawing from or suspending the operation of a treaty under the provisions of the Convention. These procedural requirements were as follows:

(*a*) A party making any such claim or allegation must notify the other parties, indicating the measures which it proposed to take with respect to the treaty and the grounds therefor.

[64] *Supra*, p. 123.

(*b*) If no party had raised objection within a period of three months (an exception being made for cases of special urgency) the party making the notification might carry out the measure which it had proposed.

(*c*) If objection were raised by any other party, the parties 'shall seek a solution through the means indicated in Article 33 of the Charter of the United Nations'.

(*d*) Without prejudice to the rules on acquiescence, a State which had not previously made a notification was not precluded from doing so in answer to another party claiming performance of the treaty or alleging its violation.

The draft article contained, in addition, a clause saving the rights or obligations of the parties under any provisions in force binding the parties with regard to the settlement of disputes.

To many governments these procedural safeguards were wholly insufficient, having regard to the 'progressive' content of many of the proposals made by the Commission as regards grounds of invalidity and termination. In written comments on the earlier (1963) draft, a number of suggestions had been made, ranging from the possibility of a reservations article whereby governments might exclude the application of the articles on invalidity and termination in relation to States which had not accepted an undertaking concerning compulsory jurisdiction or compulsory arbitration[65] to a more modest proposal that the draft articles on invalidity and termination should be capable of being invoked only against a State which had accepted the compulsory jurisdiction of the International Court of Justice if the State relying on the article were willing to submit the issue to the Court.[66] Other governmental comments had favoured a general provision conferring compulsory jurisdiction on the International Court of Justice for the settlement of disputes arising out of the series of articles on invalidity and termination of treaties. The Commission, having considered these and other comments, decided not to modify substantially the proposals which they had advanced in 1963, asserting that these proposals (which I have summarised above) 'represented the highest measure of common

[65] Comments by government of Luxembourg, reproduced in 1966 I.L.C. Reports, p. 138.

[66] Comments by United Kingdom government, reproduced in 1966 I.L.C. Reports, p. 169.

ground that could be found among Governments as well as in the Commission on this question'.[67]

It was apparent, even before the conference began, that there would be a major confrontation on the adequacy or otherwise of the Commission's proposals for settlement of disputes. Professor Briggs had already criticised the shortcomings of the Commission's proposal, particularly the inefficacy of the paragraph requiring the parties to seek a solution through the means indicated in Article 33 of the Charter.[68] The demonstrable weakness of this provision is that it does not oblige the parties to resort to any particular mode of third-party determination of the issue dividing them and puts a premium on unilateral (and inevitably self-serving) claims.

But there were formidable barriers facing those States which were determined to tighten up the provisions concerning disputes-settlement and to ensure that, as an integral part of the Convention, automatic procedures for third-party scrutiny of disputed claims of invalidity would be available.

In the first place, precedent was against them. At previous codification conferences[69] attempts to include provisions for the settlement of disputes by establishing the compulsory jurisdiction of the International Court of Justice had been defeated. In each case the protagonists of an effective disputes-settlement machinery had been unable to rally sufficient support for their proposals, and the soft alternative of an Optional Protocol for the Settlement of Disputes had been accepted *faute de mieux*. But the unsatisfactory nature of the Optional Protocol approach had become increasingly recognised:

> There was . . . no requirement that a party to the convention had also to be a party to the protocol. The inadequacy of the protocols as a substitute for compulsory requirements in the conventions themselves is demonstrated by the fact that in no case have as many as half of the parties to a convention ratified the relevant protocol.[70]

---

[67] 1966 I.L.C. Reports. p. 90.

[68] 'Procedures for establishing the invalidity or termination of treaties under the International Law Commission's 1966 draft articles on the law of treaties', 61 *A.J.I.L.* (1967), pp. 976–89.

[69] The Law of the Sea conferences (1958 and 1960) and the Vienna conferences on Diplomatic Relations (1961) and Consular Relations (1963).

[70] Kearney and Dalton, *loc. cit.*, p. 546; see also Dupuy, 'Codification et règlement' des differends: les débats de Vienne sur les procédures de règlement', 15 *Annuaire Français de Droit International* (1969), p. 72, and

A second factor inhibiting progress in this field was the well known opposition of the Soviet Union and other Eastern European countries to any form of impartial third-party determination of international disputes. This had been abundantly manifested in the discussions on the principle of peaceful settlement of disputes within the framework of the U.N. Special Committee on Principles of International Law concerning Friendly Relations and Co-operation among States.[71] This anachronistic attitude, based upon ideological convictions and upon the more extreme elements of the doctrine of State sovereignty, was regrettably sustained by a group of Afro-Asian countries, who, for other reasons, were opposed to the concept of independent and compulsory third-party determination of international disputes. Among the avowed reasons motivating this opposition on the part of certain Afro-Asian countries were (*a*) the distrust of the international judicial process following upon the controversial 1966 judgment of the International Court of Justice in the 'South West Africa' case;[72] (*b*) the expense of international judicial or arbitral proceedings and the delays involved in obtaining a decision on the merits; (*c*) the asserted lack of balance in the composition of the International Court which weighted it in favour of Western States; and (*d*) the suspicion that any judicial or arbitral tribunal would apply so-called 'traditional' international law in contrast to the 'new' international law which would be responsive to the needs of newly independent States.

These were indeed formidable obstacles to overcome. There was yet another with a certain superficial attraction. It was argued that the process of codification of norms of substantive international law should not be made dependent upon the development of procedural or institutional devices to secure their proper application; otherwise, it was suggested, the development of the international legal order as a whole would be placed in jeopardy.[73] But the response to this

Briggs, 'The Optional Protocol of Geneva (1958) and Vienna (1961, 1963) concerning the compulsory settlement of disputes' in *Hommage à Paul Guggenheim* (1968), pp. 640–1.

[71] See Houben, 'Principles of international law concerning friendly relations and co-operation among States', 61 *A.J.I.L.* (1967), pp. 710–16, and Rosenstock, *loc. cit.*, pp. 725–6.

[72] *I.C.J. Reports* (1966), p. 6.

[73] *Official Records, First Session,* 52nd meeting (Yasseen) and 54th meeting (Rosenne).

was quite simply that a group of States were not prepared to engage in the far-reaching and ambitious programme of progressive development represented by the Commission's proposals on invalidity and termination of treaties without a parallel advance in the field of procedures:

> If . . . the world was not yet ready to adopt the necessary procedures for dealing with the legal questions that might arise out of the provisions codified by the convention on the law of treaties, there was good reason for asking whether the world was really ready for the degree of codification embodied in the draft convention.[74]

Against this background, a variety of proposals were presented to the Vienna conference designed to strengthen the arrangements for the settlement of disputes. Of these, the most far-reaching was a proposal by Switzerland for a general article providing for the compulsory jurisdiction of the International Court of Justice in relation to all disputes concerning the interpretation or application of the Convention, unless the parties agreed to submit the dispute to arbitration.[75] This proposal was rejected, at the committee stage of the second session of the conference, by forty-eight votes to thirty-seven, with twenty abstentions.

Most of the proposals for strengthening the machinery for the settlement of disputes were, however, confined to disputes concerning the interpretation or application of the series of articles in Part V of the Convention, and in fact involved amendments or additions to the Commission proposal designed to spell out the procedure to be followed in cases where objection is raised to a notification.

Prominent among these was a Japanese proposal providing that disputes concerning claims under the *jus cogens* articles should be referred to the International Court at the instance of any party to the dispute and that, in other cases, the dispute should be referred to a simple form of arbitration if no solution had been reached within twelve months of the notification.[76]

A Swiss proposal required the notifying party to refer any claim to which objection had been raised to the International Court of Justice or to an arbitral tribunal; it was accompanied by a presump-

[74] *Official Records, Second Session,* 25th plenary meeting (Vallat).
[75] A/Conf.39/C.1/L.250.
[76] A/Conf.39/C.1/L.339 (1968).

tion of abandonment of the claim in the event of non-recourse within a prescribed period to one or other of these instances.[77]

Coming down the scale, a thirteen-power amendment, sponsored by a mixed group of Western, Latin American and Afro-Asian States,[78] embodied a two-stage procedure involving initially an institutionalised form of conciliation, followed, in the event of failure of the conciliation process, by a simple form of arbitration.

A United States proposal followed somewhat similar lines, although it envisaged the establishment of a special Commission on Treaty Disputes and contained particular provisions about allegations of material breach.[79]

Finally, a complicated Uruguayan amendment seemed designed to bring into play the powers of the Security Council and the General Assembly in relation to disputes about the invalidity or termination of treaties.[80]

The debates at the first session of the conference failed to resolve this issue. As anticipated, the Soviet Union and other Eastern European countries, supported by a number of influential Afro-Asian States, resolutely opposed all efforts to improve the disputes-settlement machinery. Nonetheless, there was discernible a growing measure of support for some additional provision along the lines of the thirteen-power proposal. In the event, however, it was decided to defer until the second session consideration of all proposals for additions to the basic Commission proposal on disputes-settlement machinery; as a result of a certain amount of tactical manoeuvring on the part of the Soviet Union and their associates, a link had been established between disputes-settlement and the 'all States' issue,[81] despite the fact that there was no logical connection between the two issues.

During the interval between the first and second sessions of the conference there was a certain amount of diplomatic activity.[82] This enabled the participants in the conference to assess with greater

[77] A/Conf.39/C.1/L.347 (1968).

[78] A/Conf.39/C.1/L.352/Rev.1 (1968), sponsored by the Central African Republic, Colombia, Dahomey, Denmark, Finland, Gabon, the Ivory Coast, Lebanon, Madagascar, the Netherlands, Peru, Sweden and Tunisia.

[79] A/Conf.39/C.1/L.355 (1968).

[80] A/Conf.39/C.1/L.343 (1968).

[81] This is, in effect, the highly political issue of which entities whose status is in dispute constitute 'States'; it is normally advanced, with becoming innocence, as an application of the principle of universality.

[82] Kearney and Dalton, *loc. cit.*, pp. 549–50.

precision the likely reactions to particular proposals. It appeared that the proposal which was likely to command most support at the conference would be along the lines of the thirteen-power proposal tabled at the first session. Accordingly, when debate was resumed on the issue of disputes settlement at the second session, attention was concentrated on a revised version of the thirteen-power proposal which attracted six additional co-sponsors—Austria, Bolivia, Costa Rica, Malta, Mauritius and Uganda. The nineteen-power proposal was duly adopted in the Committee of the Whole by a vote of fifty-four in favour, thirty-four against and fourteen abstentions after the anticipated defeat of the Swiss and Japanese proposals.

Meanwhile decisions on separate, and formally unconnected, issues had an influence on the final *dénouement* of the drama in plenary. First, the Committee of the Whole adopted a new article (now Article 4 of the Convention) which makes it quite clear that the Convention is strictly prospective and applies only to treaties concluded by States after the entry into force of the Convention for such States.[83] The genesis of this article is interesting. A close study of the records of the Vienna conference will reveal how the attitudes of many States towards particular proposals were influenced, and in some cases distorted, by the contemplated effect upon existing treaty disputes. In particular the divisions among Latin American States on some of the draft articles proposed by the Commission and on amendments tabled to those draft articles are in large measure attributable to the anticipated impact of the Convention upon existing disputes—particularly territorial disputes where the validity or continued operation of an old treaty might be in question. None of this is apparent on the record, as the debates at Vienna were generally conducted on an abstract level; but it requires no great knowledge of the details of current territorial disputes to see how particular delegations sought to obtain advantage for themselves by fervent support of Commission proposals or of amendments which would support their position in current treaty disputes. Another aspect of this not unexpected trend was that many States involved in existing treaty disputes were anxious lest the automatic disputes-

[83] The wording of this article, of course, poses some difficult technical questions, since it does not provide a uniform rule. How it will apply in relation to future multilateral treaties remains to be seen, since it is difficult to see how the Convention can be fully operative in relation to some parties only to such a treaty; see Schwarzenberger, *International Law and Order*, p. 54.

settlement machinery to which they were not necessarily opposed in principle might be invoked in relation to such disputes. By the second session, it had become clear that the conference would reject the vast majority of amendments and proposals which had been motivated by a desire to obtain an advantage in relation to existing treaty disputes. Accordingly, there was growing support for a specific provision about the non-retroactive effect of the Convention as a whole, particularly because this would ensure that any automatic disputes-settlement machinery would not apply to disputes arising out of existing treaties.

The second factor which influenced the final outcome was the defeat, in the Committee of the Whole, of a series of related proposals designed either to incorporate the principle that 'all States' have the right to participate in general multilateral Conventions or to ensure that the Vienna Convention itself would be open to participation by 'all States'. The first of these proposals was objected to on the ground that it ran contrary to the principle that States are, and should be, free to choose their treaty partners, the second on the ground that it raised all too familiar problems of application—who was to determine which entities whose status was in dispute were 'States'? The political overtones of those proposals were evident; they are customarily designed to achieve recognition for such entities as East Germany.[84]

So matters stood when the decisive plenary stage began. In the course of consideration in plenary of the series of articles setting out substantive grounds of invalidity and termination of treaties, a number of delegations, including those of the United States, Canada, Greece, Norway, New Zealand, the United Kingdom, the Federal Republic of Germany and Denmark, made general statements declaring that their positive support for, or abstention on, individual articles in Part V of the Convention was conditional on there being included in the Convention something on the lines of the nineteen-power amendment for automatically available disputes-settlement machinery. Other delegations, including those of Italy, the Netherlands, Senegal, Austria, Ireland and Japan made the same point in the narrower context of the *jus cogens* article.

It was thus evident that the success or failure of the conference as a whole hung on the decision which would have to be taken

[84] Kearney and Dalton, *loc. cit.*, p. 549: Rosenne, *op. cit.*, pp. 82–4.

in plenary on the nineteen-power proposal. For the nineteen-power proposal to be definitely adopted, a two-thirds majority was required. When the decisive moment came, however, the nineteen-power proposal for a new Article 62 *bis* received only sixty-two votes in favour, with thirty-seven against and ten abstentions. It therefore failed of adoption.[85]

There remained only six days before the closure of the conference. All seemed lost. Renewed efforts on the part of the Eastern European countries to incorporate a substantive article declaring that 'all States' have the right to participate in general multilateral Conventions were decisively rejected. There seemed to be total deadlock, given the undoubted determination of the Western States to secure adequate disputes-settlement machinery and the strong insistence of the Soviet Union and other Eastern European countries that some gesture should be made on the 'all States' issue. Informal meetings among leading delegations failed to move the log-jam. Numerous compromise formulae were floated, but the positions were too far apart to permit of the gap being bridged in a manner that would be positively satisfactory to all.

In these circumstances, a group of Afro-Asian countries, consisting of Ghana, the Ivory Coast, Kenya, Kuwait, Lebanon, Morocco, Nigeria, Sudan, Tunisia and Tanzania, decided to make a last-ditch attempt. They drew up a 'package' proposal consisting of a new article entitled 'Procedures for judicial settlement, arbitration and conciliation' coupled with a declaration on 'universal participation' in the Convention which in substance invited the General Assembly to give consideration, at its twenty-fourth session, to the matter of issuing invitations to States not members of the United Nations or any of its specialised agencies to become parties to the Convention.[86]

The new article, which now appears as Article 66 of the Convention, is based largely on the nineteen-power proposal, but it borrows some elements from the Japanese amendment. Thus it permits any party to a dispute concerning the interpretation or application of the *jus cogens* articles to submit that dispute to the International Court of Justice if no solution has been reached within

[85] *Official Records, Second Session*, 27th plenary meeting (16 May 1969).

[86] The General Assembly have not yet taken any action on this declaration, consideration of the matter having been deferred as a result of decisions taken at the twenty-fourth and twenty-sixth sessions.

twelve months by use of the procedures in Article 33 of the Charter and unless the parties have agreed instead to refer the issue to arbitration. For the rest, it establishes machinery for compulsory conciliation, at the instance of any party, in relation to disputes concerning the interpretation or application of the other articles in Part V of the Convention. The detailed conciliation machinery is set out in an annex to the Convention. The following are the main features of the conciliation machinery:

(*a*) Every State which is a member of the United Nations or a party to the Convention nominates two qualified jurists as conciliators. The names of the persons so nominated are included in a list to be maintained by the Secretary-General of the United Nations.

(*b*) When the conciliation machinery is invoked under Article 66, the Secretary-General brings the dispute before a conciliation commission. The State or States constituting one of the parties to the dispute is entitled to appoint:

(i) One conciliator of the nationality of that State or of one of those States who may or may not be chosen from the list.

(ii) One conciliator of the nationality of that State or of one of those States, who shall be chosen from the list.

The State or States constituting the other party to the dispute is entitled to appoint two conciliators in the same way. The four conciliators appoint, within a specified period, a fifth conciliator from the list, who acts as chairman. Any appointment not made within the specified time periods will be made by the Secretary-General.

(*c*) The conciliation commission so constituted decides its own procedure, but makes decisions or recommendations by majority vote of its members.

(*d*) The conciliation commission hears the parties, examines the claims and objections and makes proposals to the parties with a view to reaching an amicable settlement of the dispute.

(*e*) The commission is obliged to report within twelve months of its constitution. Its report is deposited with the Secretary-General and transmitted to the parties to the dispute. The report, including any conclusions regarding the facts or questions of law, is not binding upon the parties and has no other character than that of recommendations submitted for the consideration of the parties in order to facilitate an amicable settlement of the dispute.

A number of minor technical criticisms can be made of this conciliation machinery.[87] In particular, there may, on occasions, be difficulty in determining on which side of a dispute a particular State falls, in circumstances where the dispute involves more than two States. But it should equally be noted that the Annex is so constructed as to ensure that a conciliation commission will be constituted even if one of the parties to the dispute fails to appoint its conciliators within the time limit stipulated; thus the difficulties which were experienced in establishing the Treaty Commissions under the peace treaties with Bulgaria, Hungary and Romania and which gave rise to a request for an advisory opinion from the International Court of Justice[88] are effectively overcome.

Apart from these technical points, the Annex betrays some of the stresses and strains which were operative in the closing stages of the conference. The original thirteen-power proposal and the later nineteen-power proposal had, of course, been predicated on a stage of compulsory arbitration if the conciliation procedures had failed to achieve a settlement. Thus there was every reason for having a clear separation between flexible and essentially non-legal conciliation procedures and the fall-back possibility of formal arbitration which would of necessity involve a determination of the legal issues. But the 'package' proposal did not envisage any stage of compulsory arbitration or judicial settlement, except in relation to the *jus cogens* articles. Thus there was concern lest the legal aspects of the dispute might be overlooked in the conciliation process. For this reason the sponsors of the 'package' proposal modified to some extent the content of the nineteen-power proposal by laying additional stress on the obligation of the conciliation commission to hear argument on controverted issues of law and fact.[89]

Of course, there is one obvious gap in the Convention regime—what happens in the event of failure of conciliation? To this the Convention as such provides no answer, but it is not unreasonable to assume, despite the nominally recommendatory character of the

[87] See Rosenne, 'The settlement of treaty disputes under the Vienna Convention of 1969', 31 *Z.a.o.R.V.* (1971), pp. 48–52.

[88] See 'Interpretation of Peace Treaties with Bulgaria, Hungary and Romania case', *I.C.J. Reports* (1950), p. 65 and (second phase) *ibid.*, p. 221.

[89] Kearney and Dalton, *loc. cit.*, pp. 553–4.

conciliation commission's report, that a report favourable to the State having asserted a ground of invalidity or termination would *prima facie* justify that State in going ahead with the measure proposed, and that an unfavourable report would justify the objecting State in claiming continued performance of the treaty.[90]

CONCLUSIONS ON THE SETTLEMENT OF DISPUTES

A number of criticisms have been directed against the Convention regime on disputes-settlement. At one end of the spectrum, it is alleged that those States which were and are averse to any form of compulsory adjudication can hardly be expected to accept the principle of compulsory jurisdiction in relation to all disputes arising in the future over any and all treaties, or even to disputes arising in connection with the *jus cogens* articles.[91] To this, and to the associated doubt cast on the good faith of those advocating compulsory adjudication in the case of treaties, it can only be said that the touchstone of good faith surely lies in the willingness of States to accept in advance the obligation to submit to some form of impartial third-party machinery any unilateral claim based on the series of articles concerning the invalidity, termination and suspension of operation of treaties.

At the other end of the spectrum, doubt has been expressed as to the suitability of the Convention regime on disputes-settlement, particularly as regards the role of the International Court of Justice in relation to the *jus cogens* articles. It is maintained that the vague and uncertain language of the articles on *jus cogens* would give to the Court the power to decide, without any solid criteria, whether a norm is peremptory or not and would thus confer on it the task not simply of interpreting the law but of creating it.[92] It is also argued that a procedure of non-binding conciliation for disputes as grave as those which might arise in connection with the asserted invalidity of a treaty based on the articles concerning coercion of a State by the threat or use of force or *rebus sic stantibus* is thoroughly unsatisfactory.[93]

These arguments are *prima facie* compelling; but one must not

[90] Kearney and Dalton, *loc. cit.*, p. 555.
[91] Nahlik, *loc. cit.*, p. 755.
[92] Deleau, *loc. cit.*, p. 21.
[93] *Ibid.*, p. 22.

exaggerate their significance. In the first place, many would say that a limited degree of judicial innovation is already a feature of the jurisprudence of the International Court.[94] Others would go much further and argue positively, in the context of a discussion of the distinction between 'legal' and 'political' disputes, that the Court should take a much broader view of its functions and, in particular, should refrain from declining to exercise jurisdiction on the ground that the issue which is before it is 'political'.[95] It is not necessary to go so far as this in order to reach the conclusion that the Court should be able to perform the task conferred upon it by Article 66 of the Convention without indulging in overt judicial law-making. The Court may well in this context have to determine the precise significance of the expression 'the international community of States as a whole'. But beyond this, its function will be the predictable and normal function of any tribunal, that is to say, the weighing and assessment of evidence—in this case, evidence as to whether a particular rule of international law is accepted and recognised by the international community as a whole as being a norm of *jus cogens*. The task will undoubtedly be a difficult one, but it is a task which is essentially judicial in nature.

One must in any event bear in mind that the chief value of the automatic procedures for settlement of disputes now written into the Convention lies not in their precise content but in their mere existence. Paradoxically, the less they are utilised the more effective they will be. No State is anxious to indulge in lengthy and expensive international conciliation or litigation. This imposes a very heavy burden upon Foreign Offices and upon their legal advisers, with the outcome far from certain. What is important—what is indeed crucial—is that there should always be in the background, as a necessary check upon the making of unjustified claims, or upon the denial of justified claims, automatically available procedures for the settlement of disputes. In the absence of such procedures there would be no effective restraint upon States wishing to release themselves from inconvenient treaty obligations. This is the effective response to the other criticism that, if political relations between the States in dispute are bad, major disputes between them are unlikely

[94] Fitzmaurice, 'Judicial innovation—its uses and perils' in *Cambridge Essays in International Law* (1965), pp. 24–47.

[95] Rosalyn Higgins, 'Policy considerations and the international judicial process', 17 *I.C.L.Q.* (1968), pp. 58–84.

to be confinable within a treaty dispute context; and, if they are normal, that the habitual diplomatic and administrative processes will find solutions to them.[96] No one would seek to argue that the mere existence of the Convention procedures will prevent major treaty disputes from arising, particularly when relations between the States concerned are strained; but it is precisely to guard so far as possible against unjustified action in periods of strained relations that these safeguards have been written into the Convention. It is partly for this reason that reservations to Article 66 of the Convention or to the Annex raise such serious issues.[97]

III FINAL OBSERVATIONS ON THE CONVENTION AS A WHOLE

The Vienna Convention on the Law of Treaties, with all its flaws and imperfections, is a remarkable achievement. It will take its place as a landmark in the long history of codification and progressive development of international law. The subject-matter of the law of treaties is so diverse and so complex that the Convention does not in general seek to do more than indicate the residual rules which will apply unless the particular treaty otherwise provides or a different intention is otherwise established. But, in formulating these residual rules, the conference was able to reach agreement on technical solutions to a number of problems which have long troubled international lawyers. The major task was however to establish a proper balance between the requirement of security of treaties and the demand for recognition of newly emerging concepts, such as *jus cogens*, which might be destructive of that very security. A balance has been struck (some might say a very precarious balance), and this balance contains one element which must hearten those who continue to strive for the application of the rule of law in international affairs—namely, a renewed role for the International Court of Justice in relation to the interpretation and application of the *jus cogens* articles.

One final thought. The Vienna Convention on the Law of Treaties must be seen in its proper perspective, as one of the essential foundations of the codification and progressive development of international law. Failure of the codifying effort, after so much

[96] Rosenne, 31 *Z.a.o.R.V.* (1971), p. 61.
[97] *Supra*, pp. 46–50.

preparatory work involving notable contributions by the four successive British Special Rapporteurs, would have constituted a severe setback to the long-term programme for codification upon which the International Law Commission, with the support of the General Assembly, is now engaged. It is perhaps not going too far to say that the success of the Vienna Conference on the Law of Treaties, despite the formidable difficulties confronting it, was a necessary precondition for the continuance of an effective long-term codification programme. The prominent role played by many members of the International Law Commission at the conference is sufficient testimony to the importance which the Commission itself attached to the codification and progressive development of the law of treaties.

The future role to be played by the Convention now lies in the hands of governments. The Convention will not enter into force until thirty-five States have deposited instruments of ratification or accession with the Secretary-General of the United Nations. Several years may elapse before this happens. To date, six States (including the United Kingdom) have deposited instruments of ratification and eight States instruments of accession.[98] So there is still a long way to go. Whatever may be the fate of the Convention, however, its impact and influence on the treaty-making practices of governments will be (and indeed already is) considerable. In a very real sense the Convention represents a massive investment of intellectual energy and ingenuity on the part of members of the International Law Commission and of governmental representatives; let us hope that the investment will soon begin to pay dividends.

[98] As of 12 June 1972, Nigeria, Jamaica, Yugoslavia, Barbados, the United Kingdom and New Zealand had deposited instruments of ratification; Syria, Canada, Tunisia, Niger, the Central African Republic, Paraguay, Lesotho and Spain had deposited instruments of accession.

ARTICLES OF THE CONVENTION CITED IN THE TEXT

INDEX